The
Desires of
a Woman's Heart

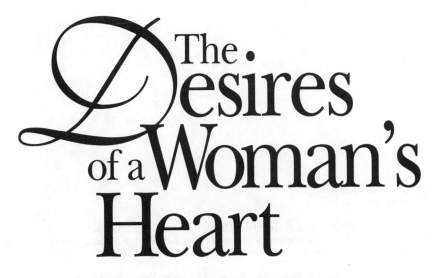

The Desires of a Woman's Heart

ENCOURAGEMENT FOR WOMEN WHEN TRADITIONAL VALUES ARE CHALLENGED

Beverly LaHaye

President, *Concerned Women for America*

Tyndale House Publishers
Wheaton, IL 60189

© 1993 by Beverly LaHaye
All rights reserved

The *"NIV"* and *"New International Version"* trademarks are registered in the United States Patent and Trademark Office by International Bible Society. Use of either trademark requires the permission of International Bible Society.

All Scripture quotations, unless otherwise noted, are from the *Holy Bible,* New International Version®. Copyright © 1973, 1978, 1984 by International Bible Society. Used by permission of Zondervan Publishing House. All rights reserved.

Scripture quotations marked NKJV are from The New King James Version of the Bible. Copyright © 1979, 1980, 1982, Thomas Nelson Inc., Publishers.

Scripture quotations marked NASB are taken from the *New American Standard Bible,* © 1960, 1962, 1963, 1968, 1971, 1972, 1973, 1975, 1977 by the Lockman Foundation. Used by permission.

Scripture quotations marked KJV are from the *Holy Bible,* King James Version.

Library of Congress Cataloging-in-Publication Data

LaHaye, Beverly.
    The desires of a woman's heart : encouragement for women when
traditional values are challenged / Beverly LaHaye.
        p.   cm.
    Includes bibliographical references.
    ISBN 0-8423-7945-2
    1. Women—Religious life.   2. Christian life–1960-   I. Title.
BV4527.L254   1993
248.8′43—dc20   93-12911

Printed in the United States of America

99   98   97   96   95   94   93
 7   6   5   4   3   2   1

*This book is lovingly dedicated to the special women in my life:
my two daughters, Linda Murphy and Lori Scheck;
my two granddaughters, Jenny Murphy and Emily Scheck;
and my daughter by marriage, Sharron LaHaye.
Each in her own way has enriched my life and helped to fulfill the
desires of my heart. Best of all, we will spend eternity together with
our best friend, the One who fulfills the desires of all our hearts,
Jesus Christ.*

Acknowledgments

This book is the result of a fine team that planned, worked, and prayed together to bring it about. I wish to acknowledge my deep gratitude to all who have made a contribution to my life and to this project—

- My husband, Tim, who serves as my sounding board, my best friend, and my greatest supporter; and one who fulfills the desires of my heart.

- My mother, Nell, who is now in heaven with the Savior she loved so dearly. She made the early sacrifices to give me the best start in life a person could desire.

- Catherine Boehme, who for several months gathered the research and documentation needed to pull the important facts together for this project.

- Angela Elwell Hunt, who contributed much by researching, organizing, and editing.

- Marian Kelley, who assisted with the tedious job of editing and proofing the material.

- Kelly Gegner, my faithful assistant, who was available to keep the computer busy, answer mail, serve coffee, answer phone calls, and fill the gaps for me in many ways.

Thanks also go to my fine staff at Concerned Women for America, who literally stayed clear of my office during the final high-pressure weeks of finishing this book.

Contents

Notes

WHAT *ARE* THE $\mathcal{D}$ESIRES OF OUR HEARTS?

Come Walk with Me . . .

If we could interview all women who have ever lived or are now living, would we be able to come up with a simple answer to the question, What are the desires of a woman's heart?

The personalities, backgrounds, and circumstances of women are so diverse that we would doubtless hear a myriad of answers. But if we examine the answers carefully, we will discover common threads woven throughout the fabric of womanhood. There are some things we all desire.

You may be a single woman who enjoys her independence and opportunity, yet you may struggle with loneliness and the desire to share your life with another. Or perhaps you are married, but you often envy the single woman's freedom and independence. Marriage may not be all that you thought it would be. Even if you have a good marriage, does it provide all you really want from life? If God has graced you with motherhood, do you still find your heart searching for some missing quality?

What are the desires of *your* heart? What do *you* want from life?

As I've thought about the many burdens, blessings,

wishes, hopes, challenges, and dreams Christian women face, I have struggled to come up with a nice, neat answer for what women want from life. Women are not monolithic. Our innermost beings are as unique as our individual fingerprints. Nevertheless, we share certain desires. This book is about our common interests and the competing voices that attempt to guide us as we seek to fulfill our desires.

THE FIRST WOMAN, EVE

The doubts flooded her mind, but he was *so* convincing. He said she wouldn't die, but that she would know all things. She'd be like God. Oh yes, God had said she and Adam could eat of any tree in the garden except this one, but would taking one little bite be so bad? And yes, God had given them dominion over all the other land and animals and life in this garden paradise—why should this tree alone stand outside the boundary of their freedom?

You can be like God. God's command had been clear, but Satan's voice, coming from the serpent, won Eve over. His logic appeared sound, and as Eve brought that forbidden fruit to her lips, she knew her life would change forever.

Eve wanted to be like God; she wanted a change from the usual—freedom from the boundaries God had placed around her. It's easy to judge Eve harshly and wonder why on earth she fell for Satan's outlandish lie. But what forbidden fruit are twentieth-century women munching on?

The lies offered to women today are not much different from the falsehood Eve heard on that warm day in the Garden. Satan appeared as a serpent that day; today he uses everything from advertising gimmicks to manicured political activists to tell women how they should think, act, and dress. We have been told that we have a "right" to make choices of life and death, of sexual life-styles, and of careers that will enable us to "have it all." We have been told that our children should be free to express their sexual desires without our judgment or restraint. We have been told that we can be like God.

The lies are subtle, aren't they? Like Eve, we may not be content with our situation and the boundaries God has placed around us. We've listened to the voices of deceit and wondered who or what we could be. We have picked forbidden fruit in a vain attempt to find out who we are.

What do you really desire? Maybe you're one of the thousands of busy women who would give their right arm for just a quiet hour with no interruptions or demands. But beyond that, do you know what you want and how to find it?

What do women really desire? Sigmund Freud said, "Despite my thirty years of research into the feminine soul, I have not yet been able to answer the great question that has never been answered: What does a woman want?"[1]

If we took a poll asking that question, I'm sure the answers would be as varied as women themselves. Some would say they want a man who will respect and love them; some might say they want a successful career. Others would probably exclaim that they want it all, and they can have it because they are super women!

THE MISSING INGREDIENT

In the last twenty-five years, we've seen millions of women caught up in the desperate act of searching for something to make their lives complete. Not knowing how to describe this nebulous search for a mysterious something, they say they are searching for themselves. How did they ever become lost?

Throughout history, generations of women have struggled to gain more freedom and recognition for their achievements. Many battles for women's rights were beneficial. When the law of the land dictated that women didn't deserve a voice in our elections, the women's suffrage movement fought to give women that voice. When female work-

ers earned less for the same job than men did, the Equal
Employment Opportunity Act of 1972 prohibited all sex discrimination in hiring, pay, and promotion.

But in recent days, the battles have changed. Calls for
more "rights" have increased. Women have gained a new
voice, but is that voice really helping women?

Feminists have promised women happiness and significance in a land free of gender distinction, but further
advances in the area of women's "rights" could result in
curses upon women and society as a whole. For example,
laws that require a husband to support his wife and children financially would be moot in a gender-free society.
Some of these laws have already been changed—to the detriment of women.

In 1973, for instance, the Colorado state legislature
amended an existing law that required a husband to support his wife and children, changing "sexist" words such as
man, woman, husband, and *wife,* into "sex-neutral" words.
Now the law states that a person must support a spouse.[2]
Not only does this law not support women; in many cases it
may obligate them! Already the feminist agenda has helped
ruin the marriages, families, and careers of women of all
ages, classes, and races.

I keep asking myself: After twenty-five years of this "freedom" that the feminist agenda has brought us, why do
women still struggle and search for meaning to their lives?
Why are single-parent families the fastest-growing segment
of the poor in our society? Why does the divorce rate continue to climb?

I believe we are entering a new phase in American culture. We are learning, slowly, that maybe all this freedom
for women hasn't brought us very far. In her book *Women:
Beyond Equal Rights,* Dee Jepsen writes, "It seems that one
myth has been exchanged for another. First the ideal of
marriage, home, and family was to bring idyllic bliss. Now

careers, education, power and serving 'self' will produce a full and happy life. Neither is true."[3]

What do Christian women really want? Many things: We want to honor our God in our personal and spiritual lives. We want to reflect his principles and truths in our families. We want to have an impact upon our world.

My hope is that in this book we can look at God's time-honored truths and see that they are as applicable today as they were thousands of years ago. We will see that women don't need to be redefined or "overhauled"—God has given us clear direction to allow us to be light in an ever-changing world. As Satan continues in his fight against truth, we must stand ready. We can choose to stand according to God's truths or fall prey to Satan's lies.

As Jesus said in John 10:10, "The thief comes only to steal and kill and destroy; I have come that they may have life, and have it to the full."

Walk with me as we discover the abundant life God has planned especially for women.

DESIRES IN OUR PERSONAL LIFE

1

We Want Happiness and Significance

What is the number one desire of your heart? What do you want more than anything else? Most women, if given five seconds to answer those questions, will say, "Happiness."

Every human being, whether male or female, has an innate, relentless drive to be happy. In his book *The Pursuit of Happiness: Who Is Happy—and Why?* social psychologist David G. Myers notes that happiness is what people seek above all else:

> When we pit happiness against many things that we long for—robust health, social respect, large incomes—most of us choose happiness. Indeed, our search for happiness and for relief from misery motivates a host of behaviors, from success seeking to sex to suicide.[1]

Blaise Pascal, the seventeenth-century Christian philosopher and mathematician, would have agreed:

> All men seek happiness. This is without exception. Whatever different means they employ, they all tend to

this end. The cause of some going to war, and of others avoiding it, is the same desire in both, attended with different views. The will never takes the least step but to this object. This is the motive of every action of every man, even of those who hang themselves.[2]

Anne Frank said, "We all live with the objective of being happy; our lives are all different and yet the same."[3]

C. S. Lewis became a Christian as a result of his "longing for joy, a joy that does not reside in any earthly object that seems to promise it."[4]

When we struggle in a trying situation, we are groping for a resolution—a sense of peace, fulfillment, contentment, and joy. We want to be happy.

WHERE DOES HAPPINESS COME FROM?

Since Charles M. Schulz defined happiness as a "warm puppy," and Pascal says it is the motive of every action of man, it should be obvious that we all have different criteria for what we mean by happiness. *Webster's Dictionary* defines it as a "state of well-being and contentment; a pleasurable satisfaction." When we're happy, we feel alive, positive, optimistic, exhilarated, inspired, motivated, and joyful.

Happiness does not always depend upon circumstances. Remember the story of Scrooge in *A Christmas Carol?* Scrooge's circumstances did not change the morning he awoke after his Christmas Eve dream, but his outlook did. For the first time in years, Scrooge was happy.

It is possible to be happy without having perfect health. Joni Eareckson Tada, though confined to a wheelchair for the rest of her life, is still able to exude happiness. I have rheumatoid arthritis, and some days the pain is quite severe. Thank goodness my happiness doesn't come from my joints, but from my heart.

My heart is affected by the thoughts I entertain, and Philippians 4:8 gives a positive formula for the thoughts that bring happiness: "Whatever is true, whatever is noble, whatever is right, whatever is pure, whatever is lovely, whatever is admirable—if anything is excellent or praiseworthy—think about such things."

But happiness is a mysterious commodity. The harder we pursue it, the faster it escapes us.

The ancient Greeks said a life of peaceful and intelligent contemplation would lead to happiness. The Epicureans' variation on this theme was that happiness was found in enjoying life's pleasures. The Stoics taught that happiness followed virtuous attitudes.

In our day we hear that happiness comes from doing what we want, when we want, with whom we want, with the freedom or ability to escape the inevitable consequences. For example, look at the way our tragic society has so easily accepted abortion on demand. Our acceptance of what was unthinkable two generations ago shows our modern commitment to removing the consequences of our actions. Abortion is legal, supposedly, for the sake of our happiness.

Feminists tell us that what makes women happy is "justice for their gender, not wedding rings and bassinets."[5] Who would argue against the necessity of justice? But to argue that the majority of women dream of justice for their gender more than babies and the security of home and a loving marriage is more than a little farfetched.

Feminists also assert that women yearn for the freedom to "define themselves—instead of having their identity defined for them."[6] In their fierce independence, feminists want to shrug off all authority, regardless of the source. This includes, of course, men, government, culture, and God.

According to feminists, justice for their gender and self-definition are two prerequisites to women's happiness. Groping for happiness outside the will of God, feminists nurse a bitterness toward anyone who encroaches on their "rights" of equality and self-rule. These women are enslaved to the notion that independence, indulgence, a self-centered orientation to life, and the fleeting pleasure of recognition will provide women with the sense of well-being for which they relentlessly long.

In the last twenty years, feminists have obtained much of what they want. But are they happy?

HAPPINESS AND PAYCHECKS

Magazines, newspapers, television, and film abound with the message that money brings happiness and power. Every day we are assaulted with the image of thin, pretty women behind executive desks with fax machines demanding their immediate attention. Feminists would have you believe that you'll be happier behind that desk, with more income and more power. If something costs a little more, it's okay—you're earning your own money, and as a woman, you're "worth it"!

In the Bible, however, Jesus instructs us to "watch out! Be on your guard against all kinds of greed; a man's life does not consist in the abundance of his possessions" (Luke 12:15). Jesus did not give us this warning to lessen our joy; on the contrary, his love for us led him to expose the emptiness of materialism. When we stray from the direction that gives true happiness, God lovingly restores us and guides us back to the path of righteousness.

I think too many of us consider Jesus' instruction about material possessions a mere pious platitude. We are quick to judge happiness by what we see in earthly possessions. We know families who live in big houses, who summer on the lake with expensive ski boats, or who vacation in exotic locales, and we assume they are happier than we are. We don't see their problems. Thousands of "successful" couples fall into bed at night without speaking. They're too tired, they're too busy, and their minds aren't on each other but on the pressures that surround them.

Let's compare Jesus' teaching with what Dr. Myers discovered in his studies about happiness:

> Over time, does our happiness grow with our paychecks? . . . In the United States as a whole, the answer is clearly no. Since the 1950's, our buying power has doubled. . . . In 1990, as in 1957, only one in three Americans told the University of Chicago's National Opinion Research Center they were 'very happy.' So: *We're twice as rich—not just 20 percent richer—yet we're no happier.*[7]

Psychologists have found that once a person is above poverty level, an increase in wealth will not significantly improve his or her morale. Certainly wealth can buy opportunity, but the danger of the allure of wealth is its tendency to possess the possessor. Paul says those who are rich should not be arrogant or put their hope in wealth, but "in God, who richly provides us with everything for our enjoyment" (1 Timothy 6:17). Paul further encourages the wealthy to be rich in good works: "But godliness with contentment is great gain. For we brought nothing into the world, and we can take nothing out of it" (1 Timothy 6:6-7).

Related to the idea that a fat paycheck brings happiness is the idea that independence from restricting relationships leads to happiness. Feminists reason that mothers waste their precious educations and intellect when they opt to stay home with their growing children. Women who choose to support a husband in his career and life goals are viewed as failures, for they have neglected to advance themselves.

Why do feminists place such emphasis on self? Self-preoccupation does not advance happiness. Quite the opposite! According to Dr. Myers,

Rampant individualism carries with it two seeds of its own destruction. First, a society that exalts the individual to the extent ours does now will be ridden with depression. . . . Second, and perhaps most important, is meaninglessness [which occurs when there is no] attachment to something larger than you are."[8]

THE PARADOX OF HAPPINESS

It is clear that Western society has not reached a consensus on what the source of happiness is. One thing we do know, however, is that we need to be happy because happiness has a direct effect on our physical well-being. Dr. Myers writes that "emotions are biological events": Our bodies' immune systems fight disease more effectively when we are happy. He concludes that "human happiness is both an end—better to live fulfilled, with joy—and a means to a more caring and healthy society."[9]

I found Dr. Myers' study on happiness fascinating because it dispels many of the myths about what truly makes people happy. "Wealth-accumulating materialism and self-focused individualism do not produce the hoped-for-well-being. . . . Active spirituality and close relationships such as marriage do enhance well-being."[10]

Dr. Myers' findings remind me of the two great commandments Jesus gave to the young lawyer who put him to the test. The lawyer asked, "Teacher, which is the greatest commandment in the Law?" Jesus replied: "'Love the Lord your God with all your heart and with all your soul and with all your mind.' This is the first and greatest commandment. And the second is like it: 'Love your neighbor as yourself'" (Matthew 22:36-39).

In other words, the two most important commandments are to maintain an active relationship with God and to do the same with other people. Why does God give us commandments to obey? So that we will be happy.

It is unscriptural, however, to seek our personal happiness directly. In fact, we are told that if we want to find our lives (find happiness in life), we must first lose our lives (Matthew 16:25). This is quite a paradox, one that would be incomprehensible to women of a feminist mind-set. Fortunately, its truth is not diminished by unbelief.

Happiness is not a goal to be sought, but the by-product of a life in obedience to God. We can't have it any other way. The world, the flesh, and the devil would have you "enjoy now, pay later." It takes conviction and stamina to resist such an offer, for it caters to our society's bent toward immediate gratification.

God's way, in stark contrast to the self-centered, grab-it-now philosophy of our world, is that of delayed gratification but ultimate fullness of joy. There is joy in obedience. God's payment plan is, "Buy now, enjoy now and always." When we do what is right, we have contentment, peace, and happiness. No amount of money or power can simulate the deep contentment and security of a person who is right with God and others.

What is the root of happiness? Knowing and obeying God. God wants each of his children to be happy. As Jesus reminded his disciples, if we ask our heavenly Father for a piece of bread, he will not give us a stone (Matthew 7:9-11). On the contrary, the Lord is gracious to us; he has compassion on us.

HAPPINESS AND DOING RIGHT

Happiness is the incentive that God often gives us when encouraging us to live righteously.

In the fourth chapter of Genesis we can read about an encounter between God and Cain. God had been pleased with the offering Cain's brother, Abel, had brought to him, but God had rejected Cain's offering of the fruit of the ground, and Cain was not very happy. God asked Cain, "Why are you angry? Why is your face downcast?"

The Bible does not say why God rejected Cain's offering. Perhaps Cain's motives were not pure, or perhaps he was not acting in faith. In any case, after asking Cain the rhetorical questions concerning his anger and countenance, God instructed him: "If you do what is right, will you not be accepted? But if you do not do what is right, sin is crouching at your door; it desires to have you, but you must master it" (Genesis 4:7).

We can learn an important lesson about happiness from this passage. If we do well, we will be accepted, or, as the King James Version states, our countenances will be lifted up. In other words, happiness comes from doing what is right!

Psalm 37:3-4 is the classic passage on finding happiness and joy in doing what is right: "Trust in the LORD and do good; dwell in the land and enjoy safe pasture. Delight yourself in the LORD and he will give you the desires of your heart."

If we want to experience the desires of our hearts, God commands us to trust in him and do good. We do not have to pursue wealth or happiness or ourselves or meaning in life. God will give us what we need as a gift from him. "Every good and perfect gift is from above, coming down from the Father of the heavenly lights, who does not change like shifting shadows" (James 1:17).

Jesus told us that if we abide in him and keep his commandments, we will find joy: "I have told you this so that my joy may be in you and that your joy may be complete" (John 15:11).

We must simply remain in the Lord. One of my favorite hymns is "Trust and Obey." The chorus says: "Trust and obey, for there's no other way to be happy in Jesus, but to trust and obey."

What about you? How are you seeking happiness? Whatever your circumstances, God wants you to have a life of joy, happiness, and rich reward. Will you trust him with your past, present, and future? Will you step out in faith and obey what you know he wants you to do? God will not take advantage of you; he will never leave you or forsake you. You can *trust and obey* him with your whole heart!

I hope that wherever you are today, God will meet your needs and provide the comfort and encouragement to help you face every challenge in your life with faith and confidence in God's goodness. Remember, you're never alone. God is by your side, and he loves you. His every motive is to bless you and lead you to real, lasting happiness.

OUR NEED FOR SELF-ESTEEM
Historian Barbara Tuchman observed,

> Ours is not a time of self-esteem or self-confidence—as was, for instance, the nineteenth century, when self-esteem may be seen oozing from its portraits. Victorians, especially the men, pictured themselves as erect, noble, and splendidly handsome. Our self-image looks more like Woody Allen.[11]

If your self-image had a face of its own, would it look like a poised and confident woman or a tousled and tattered sleepyhead? I haven't always had a perfectly healthy self-image. In my many moves, I discovered a fragile, vulnerable side to my personality. In each new environment I would question where I fit in and wonder about my identity and importance there. It's like being the new kid in school—you've got to stake out your own place, and sometimes it's hard not to worry about what the teacher and the other kids are thinking about you.

As women, we want to know we are important and that

we have a significant place in our world. We need to know that we matter to someone, that our lives are making a difference in the lives of other people, that we are able to touch their souls. This desire to have value is God-given. The person who loses sight of purpose and meaning in life will develop an unhealthy attitude about herself and wander aimlessly through life.

Not long ago I read a column by William Raspberry about Robert L. Woodson, president of the National Center for Neighborhood Enterprise. Raspberry told of a discussion he had with Woodson about his twenty years of studying successful American social programs. He had discovered a common thread among them: "I'm not saying the spiritually-based programs always work," said Woodson, "only that the successful programs almost always have a spiritual base. . . . I do know that the hunger I sense in America is not a hunger for things, but a search for meaning."[12]

Self-esteem, self-image, significance, fulfillment—all these words describe a vital ingredient for happy human life. As Thomas Szasz said in his book *The Second Sin:* "As the internal-combustion engine runs on gasoline, so the person runs on self-esteem: if he is full of it, he is good for a long run; if he is partly filled, he will soon need to be refueled; and if he is empty, he will come to a stop."[13]

FALSE AVENUES TO FULFILLMENT

In his book *The Search for Significance,* Robert McGee discusses the importance of fulfillment. The craving for fulfillment is such a strong force in our lives, says McGee, that if not channeled correctly, it can be a tool for our own ruin. I have seen that this need can pressure us to live according to the whims of public opinion and the latest media fad.

For example, many women have been drastically affected by the feminists' opinion that mothers who choose to stay at home and care for their children have little significance and meaning in life. In the words of Vivian Gornick, a feminist author, "Being a housewife is an illegitimate profession."[14] Popular opinion has driven some women to attempt to lead two lives and become "super moms," only to find out that the challenge does not bring satisfaction. Instead, it confuses their priorities, shortchanges their homes and families, and totally exhausts the women themselves.

Our inner longing for self-esteem and significance begins early in life and continues until we die. From childhood, we search for people who will love us. Our desire for acceptance pressures us to perform for the praise of others. We strive for success, driving our minds and bodies harder and farther, hoping that because of our sweat and sacrifice, others will appreciate us more.

Sometimes we aren't aware of the forces that drive us. As McGee so ably points out,

> The man or woman who lives only for the love and attention of others is never satisfied—at least, not for long. Despite our efforts, we will never find lasting, fulfilling peace if we have to continually prove ourselves to others. Our desire to be loved and accepted is a symptom of a deeper need—the need that governs our behavior and is the primary source of our emotional pain. Often unrecognized, this is our need for self-worth.[15]

The need to be needed drives us all, and many of us base our self-esteem and personal significance on the care we can give to an infant, an elderly parent, a spouse, or people in our community.

I have met many young girls in the inner cities of America who, longing to feel wanted and significant, become pregnant. They reason that if they have a child, they will be needed. A baby will belong to them and give them someone to care for. A child will give them a sense of purpose, they think.

It is a sad commentary on our society, but our craving for significance often moves us to take measures that are unwise and out of sync with God's timing and design. We all hunger to make sense of our lives, but often we are weak. Temptations to seek self-fulfillment outside God's plan are plentiful. When a woman loses her sense of self-worth in her marriage, she can become vulnerable to outside temptations. Her cravings for fulfillment and recognition can drive her to make choices that provide a temporary thrill, but end in the destruction of her home. Remember the old adage about the grass always being greener on the other side of the fence? Consider this—many times people on the other side of the fence are admiring how green your grass is!

PERFORMANCE DOES NOT EQUAL FULFILLMENT

In her book *Women: Beyond Equal Rights,* Dee Jepsen writes about women who are driven to succeed:

> We have talked about women who have accomplished what they thought they were supposed to do to succeed, but in the quality of whose "success" there dwelled a sense of "failure." For success, as defined by the world, is but one aspect of the whole of life. Many women with successful worldly careers find themselves fragmented failures at life. The pursuit of a worldly illusion of success often terminates in disappointment and feelings of betrayal.[16]

Author Anne Ortlund confirms the futility of seeking success for self. She writes, "Ego keeps you forever tense and dissatisfied, forever in agony lest someone else appear better, smarter, richer, more liked, more successful, more admired, more spiritual, more 'blessed.' "[17]

Yes, even Christians can fall into the "performance equals significance" trap. We must beware of our human tendency to compare ourselves to others. Indeed, God asked the prophet Jeremiah: "Should you then seek great things for yourself? Seek them not" (Jeremiah 45:5).

God's words to Jeremiah do not mean that we should not strive to reach our full potential, but God wants to protect us from vainly pursuing accomplishments in order to achieve fulfillment. We can all name very accomplished people who still feel tense and dissatisfied.

"When women, or men, do not understand the value, dignity, and worth they have in Christ," writes Jepsen, "they try to find it elsewhere. If women buy into the cultural mindset, which some in the feminist movement present, that our jobs will make us more important, it will only be a temporary cover-up for their insecurities."[18]

Too often we look for answers in the wrong places or in the wrong manner. Our driving hunger for fulfillment and acceptance may lead us to measure our accomplishments, professional or otherwise, by comparing them to those of our neighbors or friends. This "economic" approach—inflating or deflating the worth of an accomplishment based upon others' performance—is not an effective way to evaluate the significance of a human being.

Take, for instance, the mother of Haywood Jeffries, the NFL wide receiver who plays with the Houston Oilers. Mrs. Jeffries raised seventeen children. When Haywood, her sixteenth, was a senior in college, his mother was dying of kidney disease. She went to his last four college football games in a wheelchair even though she was so ill she should not have been out of bed. Every time the national anthem played, she would touch two fingers to her forehead in a silent salute to her son. Mrs. Jeffries died before Haywood was drafted into the NFL, but now, when the national anthem is played at the Oilers' football games, Haywood Jeffries turns his face toward heaven and touches two fingers to his forehead in a salute to his mother.

Throughout his adult life, Haywood has received accolades for his athletic ability, but the recognition that has always meant the most to him was that silent salute from one special woman. His mother, who invested her life, not in a career, but in seventeen children, left her son a great legacy and a sterling example of success.

THE REAL BASIS FOR SELF-WORTH

"Few American women, it seemed to me, simply rejoice in being what they are," Pearl S. Buck once told the U.S. House of Representatives. "And because they cannot rejoice they tend to be fretful and jealous of each other. Being self-doubtful, they achieve far less than they should. And the root of all this self-doubt, which has become a part of their very natures, is to be found in their uncertainty as human beings."[19]

We need to wake up to the truth about self-esteem. Our worth is not found in what we do or what we own or what we accomplish. Our worth is found in the simple fact that we are God's redeemed creation. We are worth more than the earth, trees, animals, and all the rest of creation because God sent his Son to redeem us. God created us and he loves us. Our worth is inestimable.

As God's creation, we are conceived and born with great worth, for God does not create worthless lives. It is we who impose low self-esteem on ourselves. Consider this verse from Scripture: "For you know that it was not with perishable things such as silver or gold that you were redeemed from the empty way of life handed down to you from your forefathers, but with the precious blood of Christ, a lamb without blemish or defect" (1 Peter 1:18-19). If you ever have cause to doubt your own worth, consider the great price God paid to redeem you!

But in our increasingly godless and secular society, men and women do not understand the only real basis for self-worth. As a result, human life has become devalued and practically worthless. Many of us have convinced ourselves that aborting a child is responsible and an act of kindness. We find excuses for the doctor who helps patients commit suicide. We rationalize a case of infanticide because the child is not perfectly healthy and "wouldn't have had a good life, anyway."

Who are we to make such decisions? Our society has given men and women authority that should belong only to God, and these men and women are randomly determining which lives are valid and valuable, and which are not.

ASK THE RIGHT QUESTION

Several years ago I took note of an interesting response that Elisabeth Elliot gave to an interviewer from *Moody Monthly* magazine. She had been asked about women's changing roles and how women could answer the question Who am I? She gave a wise reply: "I think it's more important to ask, 'Whose am I?' 'Who am I?' is such a dead street. It's more worthwhile to direct our energies toward knowing God than toward knowing ourselves."[20]

Since we have been redeemed by God, pursuing significance through a career or social life is, as the author of Ecclesiastes proclaimed, "vanity of vanities!" (Ecclesiastes 1:2, NASB). Our worth and significance are given to us, and what is given does not have to be achieved or obtained.

Can I be honest a moment? We must beware of the temptation to try to earn "self-worth" points in the Christian world. I've seen many wonderful Christian women get so caught up in doing "Christian" things that they lose sight of what a relationship with Christ is really about. While there is an important place for good stewardship of what we have been given, we need to remember that we are God's workmanship. God works through us for his purposes, and it is not up to us to decide what his purposes should be!

To me, that realization is a huge relief. I don't have to buy into the feminist agenda and "be all I can be" in order to feel that I'm a worthy individual. I don't have to do *everything* in order to feel that I'm doing all God wants me to do. God has freed me from the performance trap, and I let him tell me how he wants to work in my life.

The world will laugh at the idea that faith in God can lead us to happiness, self-esteem, and significance. But while the world vainly pursues empty paths to fulfillment and success, we who know Christ realize that only in him is complete fulfillment ever found.

God's touch gives significance to everything we do. Perhaps you have struggled with the pressure of feminist rhetoric that urges you to do all, be all, and have all. Stop for a moment before instinctively reacting to this secular challenge. Consider what God has to say about your life:

> Since, then, you have been raised with Christ, set your hearts on things above, where Christ is seated at the right hand of God. Set your minds on things above, not on earthly things. For you died, and your life is now hidden with Christ in God. When Christ, who is your life, appears, then you also will appear with him in glory. (Colossians 3:1-4)

GOD'S GIFT OF HAPPINESS AND SIGNIFICANCE

I have seen this passage of Scripture beautifully illustrated in the life of my own mother. She did not have an easy life, and she experienced many hardships and trials. Over the seventy years of her married life, she buried each of her three husbands. There were lean years in the 1940s when my mother had to rely on the assistance of a welfare program. Life was tough, but she worked hard to give her four children as normal a life as she could. We never had riches, and we often wore used, made-over clothing.

But throughout those hard years, I never remember my mother feeling sorry for herself or wanting to bail out. She had set her heart and mind on "things above." She found significance through her trust in Christ.

Mom went to her heavenly reward at the age of ninety-two and is now at home with her heavenly Father. The Christian example she left behind for her children is far greater than riches or the memory of a successful career. It was her eternal values and belief in God that led me to follow in her footsteps.

I can still remember her singing one of her favorite hymns:

> Jesus is all the world to me, my life, my joy, my all;
> He is my strength from day to day, without him I
>   would fall—
> When I am sad to him I go,
> No other one can cheer me so;
> When I am sad he makes me glad,
> He's my friend.

If we have received Jesus Christ into our hearts and obtained forgiveness for our sins, we are so wonderfully blessed! Our almighty Creator longs to communicate with us and share his desires for our lives. We are important to him, and he loves us beyond measure.

Do you remember a time in your life when someone did something unusual for you? Maybe you were given a special gift on an ordinary day; perhaps flowers arrived unexpectedly, or you were surprised with an engagement ring.

Remember how important and significant that gift made you feel?

God gave us his Son as a gift of life one night in a rough stable. This priceless gift came through an ordinary village girl named Mary. I imagine her breath was taken away when she looked into the face of God and held the One who had always known the heavenly realm as home.

And I imagine the soldier who stood at the foot of the cross was breathless for a moment as he looked up into the bleeding, dying face of Jesus of Nazareth. That face, he realized, was the face of the almighty God who had knit him together in his mother's womb.

Those breathless moments when we realize our full worth are rare. More common are the occasions when we stare into the mirror and wonder where our waistlines have gone, or we visit a class reunion and speculate about why our lives don't measure up to the gal's across the room. But God calls us to bring all of our concerns and desires to him.

When you feel like the "old you" and are dwelling on your failures, meditate on the following passage of Scripture. I've found it helps pull me out of the pit of self-condemnation: "Brothers, I do not consider myself yet to have taken hold of it. But one thing I do: Forgetting what is behind and straining toward what is ahead, I press on toward the goal to win the prize for which God has called me heavenward in Christ Jesus" (Philippians 3:13-14). It's comforting to know that not even the apostle Paul had everything together in his life—but he looked forward, not backward.

We can all look *forward* and know that God calls us onward because we are important to him. God gives our lives significance, and only in God will we find happiness.

QUESTIONS
FOR REFLECTION AND DISCUSSION

1. What do you desire out of life?
2. How would you define happiness?
3. Is it unbiblical to pursue happiness?
4. What brings happiness?
5. Would women really be happier if the feminist agenda were realized?
6. What can women do to overcome the "performance equals significance" trap?
7. Why is it ultimately more important to answer the question "Whose am I?" than "Who am I"?
8. What is the source of true significance and fulfillment in a woman's life?

2

We Want Meaningful Friendships with Women

My husband and I live in a condominium in our city. Neighbors in our building hardly know each other. About the best we can get from our neighbors is a little grunted "hello" as we pass one another in the hallway or see one another in the elevator. This is not friendship, it is scarcely even community. I sometimes wonder, *How would I even know if my neighbors were in need?* I wouldn't know if they were ill or had lost a loved one, because we simply don't communicate with one another. Sadly, this situation is true of many communities. Friends are rare in many levels of society.

Western European and North American women live in what psychologists term *individualist societies*—societies that place great importance on personal identity and self-reliance rather than on group identity and solidarity with extended family and colleagues. In his book *The Pursuit of Happiness: Who Is Happy—and Why?* psychologist David Myers writes:

> People in competitive, individualist cultures, such as the United States, have more independence, make

more money, take more pride in personal achievements, are less geographically bound near elderly parents. . . . But compared to collectivists, individualists
are also lonelier, more alienated, less likely to feel
romantic love, more likely to divorce, more homicidal,
and more vulnerable to stress-related diseases such as
heart attacks.[1]

Dr. Myers notes that "social support—feeling liked,
affirmed, and encouraged by intimate friends and family—
promotes both health and happiness."[2] People with close
relationships, he says, are less likely to die prematurely than
those with few social ties. "People most at risk for illness,"
he says, "are those who experience a trauma, continue to
think about it, but don't talk about it."[3] Loneliness is a
destructive force. People who do not have someone to
whom they can pour out their heart must keep their feelings and emotions bottled up within them.

THE LONELY AMERICAN WOMAN

You and I need to make a great effort to develop
friendships, because we are swimming against a powerful
tide. Generations ago women spent a great deal of their
lives with other women as they engaged in daily tasks
related to the home, but today there is no need for us to
congregate routinely. Our independence does promote
potential and flexibility, but it also destroys many of the hidden but significant benefits of interrelated living.

Samuel Johnson spoke of "the enduring elegance of
female friendship," but most women feel isolated from
other women. Everyone is so busy these days, few have the
time to develop friendships. We're on a fast-moving tread-
mill, and as we go to work, organize and run our house-
holds, chauffeur our children, and stay busy at church, we

cut corners to save time. Along the way, we begin to neglect the women we have known as friends.

Recently a popular women's magazine published an article titled "All Alone: The New Loneliness of American Women." The writer explained that this loneliness is a by-product of a society that "pays lip service to closeness but glorifies production."[4] Our focus has moved away from caring for one another to making time for personal achievements. This sad development has become a nationwide phenomenon.

I remember the days when people enjoyed frequent fellowship. Whether it was neighbors sitting on the lawn talking, a potluck dinner at church, or a family reunion, we never considered cutting out "extra-curricular" people in our lives. We took time to linger over coffee to discuss upcoming events or interesting insights. But today, with our busy agendas and grandiose dreams, we have forgotten our friends.

We will reap what we sow. If we give time, love, and encouragement to others, we will surely receive the same in due course. We will not reap what we do not sow. The Scriptures tell us that "a generous man will prosper; he who refreshes others will himself be refreshed" (Proverbs 11:25).

THE IMPORTANCE OF FEMALE BONDING

Psychologists have observed that men need to bond with men. Similarly, women need to bond with women. From my observation, there is a certain kinship that rarely crosses the line of gender. Women tend to understand other women better than men do. This makes sense because the Scriptures teach that men and women are different in creation and purpose.

I always enjoy hearing of secular research that confirms biblical truths. I found another confirmation of God's teaching in Dr. Deborah Tannen's book, *You Just Don't*

Understand: Women and Men in Conversation. Despite the current tendency to downplay distinctions between the sexes, Dr. Tannen courageously notes the existence of inherent differences in the communication of men and women:

> There *are* gender differences in ways of speaking, and we need to identify and understand them. Without such understanding, we are doomed to blame others or ourselves—or the relationship—for the otherwise mystifying and damaging effects of our contrasting conversational styles.[5]

Dr. Tannen has observed that women typically view life as a community and conversations as "negotiations for closeness in which people try to seek and give confirmation and support, and to reach consensus." Men, on the other hand, view life as a "contest, a struggle to preserve independence and avoid failure," and conversations as "negotiations in which people try to achieve and maintain the upper hand."[6] How different we are! Certainly these are generalizations, not infallible, eternal truths. Nevertheless, I think they can assist us in understanding why it is important for women to have female friends.

Female friends tend to understand our perspectives, feelings, ideas, and ways of thinking. Generally speaking, if a woman does not receive affirmation from other women, it will be all the more difficult for her to be secure in her relationships with men. This is just one reason why it is so important for women to cultivate and maintain friendships in every season of life.

There are many different degrees and types of friendship among women. On one end of the spectrum are people with whom we are casually acquainted, and on the other end are people with whom we share our deepest feelings, confident that they will accept and love us unconditionally.

Different friends meet different needs. Naomi Rhode discusses this in her book on friendship, *More Beautiful than Diamonds:*

> Two major categories of diamonds are unearthed from the world's diamond mines—gem quality and industrial quality. Both are genuine diamonds and are valued for their unique properties. Over 80 percent of the diamonds in the world are used industrially. Only 20 percent of those being mined can be used as gems, and even fewer are large enough to be made into a jewel much larger than the head of a match.
>
> It's much the same with our friendships—we invest in and treasure a wide variety of people, but only a small percentage are our most beloved gems. That small percentage brings us the greatest reward but we couldn't live without our "industrial" friendships.[7]

FRIENDS WHO UNDERSTAND AND INSPIRE

Whatever our situation in life—whether we are single, married, divorced, or widowed—we can and should surround ourselves with friends who not only understand us, but also inspire us to make the most of our current calling. During times of need and loneliness, women can and should encourage one another to live godly lives full of faith, hope, and love.

Single women need the stability, continuity, and belonging that friendship provides. An increasing number of women are marrying later in life, if at all. These women often find that those who were once their peers are now in a different phase of life, having married and started having children. While friendships from another era often can and should be maintained, having friends who can relate to one's present circumstances is usually very beneficial.

Some may find this surprising, but wives can be among

the most lonely of women. Some women enter marriage expecting their husbands to be ever-present, loving, understanding, affectionate, compassionate companions. After the courtship and honeymoon, however, their Princes Charming have somehow been transformed into workaholics, golf fanatics, or couch potatoes. Some situations are even bleaker, such as in cases of infidelity or addiction. It is devastating for women to be abandoned by the ones to whom they gave themselves totally, without reservation.

A good, loyal, consistent friend is indispensable in a time of great need. Because women usually outlive their husbands, the prospect of widowhood is very real for women. To whom does a widow turn when she has lost her companion of many years? Once again, a true and understanding friend can be a source of great comfort and healing. Others who have been widowed are able to encourage and minister uniquely to women mourning the loss of their husbands.

In our generation we are seeing many women who suffer from the aftermath of divorce. There is also a large number of women who have had children outside of marriage. The pain of separation compounded with the taxing work of raising children can be overwhelming to many women. These women need the emotional, physical, and spiritual support that caring believers can offer them. Many churches have support groups for single parents. If we can offer to help with child care, meal preparation, house cleaning, or financial needs, we can demonstrate true friendship and love in action.

THE IMPACT OF A FRIEND

Friends are an indispensable part of a meaningful life. They are the ones who share our burdens and multiply our blessings. A true friend sticks by us in our joys and sorrows. In good times and bad, we need friends who will pray for us, listen to us, and lend a comforting hand and an understanding ear when needed.

Our friends influence us greatly. They can be a blessing or a curse, depending on who they are. As Proverbs 13:20 tells us, "He who walks with the wise grows wise, but a companion of fools suffers harm." Paul also warns us: "Do not be misled: 'Bad company corrupts good character'" (1 Corinthians 15:33). Our lives will be shaped and molded by our friends' wisdom or foolishness.

Henry Ford once said, "Your best friend is the person who brings out of you the best that is within you."[8] I'm afraid too few of us ever ask ourselves, Who are my friends? Do they encourage me and stir up love and good works? Or do my friends lead me away from following God? Friends have the power to do both.

Just because a friend is a Christian does not guarantee that she will have a good influence on your life. Many Christians are secularized. They have been lulled into the world's pattern of living and thinking and have adopted views on crucial subjects that scarcely differ from the world's secular, godless perspective.

I recently received a letter from a woman who is four months pregnant. She is being advised by her Christian friends to abort the child because of an abnormality in the child's development. She wrote that only one of her Christian friends advised her to keep the baby and entrust the future to God's all-wise, loving, capable hands.

I am so grieved when I hear stories like this. Too many Christians have lost their flavor as salt in the world, and instead of walking by faith, they are walking by their own human sight and understanding.

Sometimes our friends may actually mislead us. For this reason, you and I need to cultivate friendships with those whose lives are characterized by obedience to God. Certainly we must reach out in friendship to those who can benefit from our maturity in Christ, but we must not do so at the risk of our own spiritual well-being. We must seek first the kingdom of God and his righteousness.

What kind of influence do your friends have on your walk with God? Do they spur you on in your devotion to Christ, or do they distract you and deter you from God's purposes? You must choose companions and intimate friends who inspire and strengthen you in your faith. And, as hard as it may be, this may mean saying good-bye to friends whose effect in your life is spiritually destructive.

As you offer the gift of friendship to others, be cautious. If you are living by a committed set of godly principles and try to be a friend to everyone, your efforts may backfire. Some women will not like you or your positions. Do not compromise your convictions in order to make a friend, for the Scripture tells us that "a man of many companions may come to ruin" (Proverbs 18:24). Aristotle observed this truth and noted that "a friend to all is a friend to none."

George Washington, our first president and a man who loved and feared God, had a few words of wisdom about friendship: "Be courteous to all," he wrote in a letter, "but *intimate with a few,* and let those few be well tried before you give them your confidence. True friendship is a plant of slow growth, and must undergo and withstand the shocks of adversity before it is entitled to the appellation."[9]

FRIENDSHIP AND THE TEMPERAMENTS

My husband has written extensively on the subject of temperaments in *Spirit-Controlled Temperament* and *Why You Act the Way You Do.* I have written *Spirit-Controlled Woman,* which outlines the differences in women's temperaments. Because these books are available for more detailed study, I will not attempt to cover the material in them here, but I would like to note that one reason some of us do better than others at making friends lies in our differences of temperament. Basically, you are an introvert or extrovert, and extroverts hardly know a stranger.

An outgoing person with soaring self-esteem generally has little difficulty charging into a new arena, be it the work place, a new neighborhood, or a new church. She will make friends easily, and she may expect others to find friendship as easy to come by as she does. Not all of us, however, are extroverted, and life does not always consist of a series of successes. There are times when all of us feel unlovable, and those of us who are introverted may struggle with the issue of making friends. We like to have our protected space, and many of us enjoy being alone. We hesitate to "stick out our necks" and subject ourselves to possible rejection. Because we are hesitant, we miss opportunities for friendship.

It's a pity that we do not realize that many people would like us if they had the chance to know us! You and I have a lot to give others—our support, experience, talents, observations, concern, love, and growing knowledge of God—and you or I may be the friend someone desperately needs.

So how do we make friends?

If you tend to be introverted, do yourself a favor and reach out in love to your neighbor, coworker, and companions. You don't need to fear their response. The Bible promises us that love never fails. When you extend love to someone, you are following the example set before us in Scripture: "Dear friends, since God so loved us, we also ought to love one another" (1 John 4:11).

Whether you are introverted or extroverted, the truth is simple: You have a lot to offer in friendship. And, as Emerson said, "The only way to have a friend is to be one."[10]

THE RISK OF SACRIFICE

Friendship building can be risky business, of course. As you reveal yourself to another, you expose yourself to the real possibility that your true self will not be warmly received. Perhaps you will be betrayed by your friend. Should the risk of betrayal inhibit you from furthering a friendship? Let's look to Jesus for the answer to this question. Although he knew Judas would betray him and prepare the way for his crucifixion, Jesus reached out to Judas in friendship, even allowing Judas to betray him with a kiss.

As Christians, we need never fear rejection, because he whose opinion matters most has already declared his unchanging, steadfast love for us and undying commitment to us. Jesus Christ has set the example for us. He publicly declared, "Never will I leave you; never will I forsake you." And so, as the writer of Hebrews states boldly, "We say with confidence, 'The Lord is my helper; I will not be afraid. What can man do to me?" (Hebrews 13:6).

The biggest risk in friendship is not rejection. It is that we will be asked to sacrifice. And indeed, that is more than a risk—it is a certainty.

Charlotte Brontë said, "If we would build on a sure foundation in friendship, we must love our friends for their sakes rather than for our own."[11] Today that perspective is considered radical—not even husbands and wives enter into that kind of sacrificial relationship!

The Bible gives us many examples of self-sacrificial friendships. We see love and sacrifice in the friendships between Jonathan and David, and Naomi and Ruth, for example. We can also see modern examples of true friendship all around us.

When my older sister was four and I was two, our father died. As a widow with two young children, my mother was in great need. At that time, a loving family befriended my mother, my sister, and me. Not only did they show concern for our welfare by extending friendship, but they actually opened up their home to us for one year. They gave to us when we had nothing to offer in return. They helped my mother get a job and truly made all of us feel at home as part of their family.

My husband, Tim, has a similar background. When he was ten years old, his father died, leaving a wife, two sons, and a daughter. When friends in their church became aware of this fatherless family's need, they reached out in love. Loving relatives invited the four of them to share their two-bedroom home for nine months.

People need friendship to deal with the common daily stress of life. Friends are invaluable in times of bereavement. We also need friends who will stand by us in our other trying times—encouragers who believe in us and are committed to seeing us smile again in victory after those times when life knocks us down.

FRIENDS IN NEED

Some time ago I visited a church in California that understood the importance of friendship. During prayer time the pastor asked, "Are there any here who are unemployed?" Several people acknowledged that they had lost their jobs. The pastor then asked those seeking employment to stand before the congregation. Once they had done that, the pastor asked the congregation if any of them felt that God might want them to be a support to one of the people standing before them. Those who did were asked to join the person they would help. In very little time, each of the unemployed people was joined by someone who pledged to provide support, prayer, encouragement, and even transportation.

I was touched by this service as I watched God's people offer to meet the needs of their brothers and sisters in a practical, tangible way. It was a flesh-and-blood picture of Galatians 6:10: "Therefore, as we have opportunity, let us do good to all people, especially to those who belong to the family of believers."

Friendship is meeting another's needs in a practical way. If a person needs a listening ear or an available shoulder to cry on, a friend is emotionally available and sensitive. If a person needs a little cash to get through the month or a place to stay, a friend will seek to meet that need or find a way to have that need met. Networking is a great way to demonstrate friendship. More than one person has found a job because a friend referred another friend.

Recently I heard about a young couple who gave their car to a person in need. The husband also found a job at his workplace for an unemployed friend. Along with his wife, this man is leading a Bible study for a young mother who was recently divorced by her unfaithful husband. The wife had befriended and led this husbandless mother to Christ only months earlier. This young couple, working both individually and as a team, have given a tremendous example of loving friendship.

Friends communicate loving concern and interest. Friends reach out and take a risk. Friends look for ways they can give, meet needs, encourage, provide for, and love. As women we really need friends who bring healing to our heartaches, disappointments, and rejections. Faithful friends, like diamonds, withstand the test of time.

STRONG AS DIAMONDS

It is in the midst of trying circumstances that the best of friendships are formed. Naomi Rhode writes:

Diamonds are carbon. So is coal. So are we. The differences between the three involve structure, background, pressure, and time. Diamond, with all its inherent properties, is one of the world's simplest compounds. What's unique about a diamond is the way it's put together and the manner in which it was formed. While graphite and coal disintegrate easily and are quite soft, diamond is the hardest naturally occurring substance known. It was formed under a very special set of circumstances. *To make it takes one million pounds per square inch of pressure and 3,000 degrees Fahrenheit.* Such conditions exist naturally only at a depth 150 miles beneath the surface of the earth.

Have you ever been under so much pressure you felt buried beneath the earth? Sometimes friendships are formed when people share that special set of circumstances.[12]

Times of tremendous pressure and heat are ideal for forming priceless, enduring friendships. The death of loved ones, the pain of divorce, and the stresses of single motherhood are ideal conditions for forming relationships that are stronger and more beautiful than diamonds.

True friendships are not based on utilitarianism or selfish interest, but on love. And what is love? The thirteenth chapter of 1 Corinthians beautifully summarizes its attributes. Let's examine verses four through seven as we replace the word *love* with *a friend:*

> A friend is patient, a friend is kind. A friend does not envy, she does not boast, she is not proud. A friend is not rude, she is not self-seeking, she is not easily angered, she keeps no record of wrongs. A friend does not delight in evil but rejoices with the truth. A friend always protects, always trusts, always hopes, always perseveres.

Biblical friendship is more beautiful than diamonds. Like a diamond, a godly friendship is built to last. Unlike modern products that often break easily, and modern theories that are often quickly refuted, God's Word and his work endure forever. So do friendships centered around God.

FRIENDSHIP IS HARD WORK

What type of woman do you want to be? Do you want to be known for your wisdom, kindness, and faith, as well as for your pure and generous heart? These attributes don't develop without concerted effort and great pains. They certainly are not the norm in our world. If we know that we will become like the company we keep, it's only logical that we must spend time with people who model the characteristics we desire to cultivate in our lives.

Friendship is inconvenient, and it takes initiative. Don't simply choose a friend because she is your neighbor or because she is bored and has free time available. Be like the virtuous woman of Proverbs 31 who went out of her way to provide the best for her family. She brought food from afar and was selective. In the essential realm of friendships, how much more selective and discerning we must be!

Being a friend is hard work—it goes beyond convenience and personal benefits into the realm of inconvenience and self-sacrifice. The Bible upholds the highest standard for friends. It tells us that "a friend loves at all times" (Proverbs 17:17).

Biblical friendship stands in stark contrast to the lesser, cheaper versions of friendship. In *The New Traditional Woman,* Connie Marshner points out that feminists view relationships as dispensable. Indeed, since we live in a world where it costs as much to repair a microwave as it does to buy a new one, friends are often readily discarded in favor of "replacements." The world's philosophy does not focus on mending broken relationships, but the Bible puts before us the high standard of unconditional, consistent, faithful, true commitment as the basis for true friendship.

The biblical recipe for friendship will cost you time, tears, and energy. A friend who is committed to us will be quick to correct us when we go astray. A friend is willing to reach down and pick up a friend who has fallen. Proverbs 27:6 tells us, "Wounds from a friend can be trusted, but an enemy multiplies kisses." A friend will offer us counsel because her overriding motive is to seek our long-term good. "Perfume and incense bring joy to the heart, and the pleasantness of one's friend springs from his earnest counsel" (Proverbs 27:9).

Friends are to speak "the truth in love" (Ephesians 4:15), and a wise friend shows compassion and consideration for our sensitivities. There is a proper time and proper way to confront a friend. "The wise in heart are called discerning, and pleasant words promote instruction," Proverbs 16:21 reminds us. A friend loves us enough to tell us what we don't want to hear in a way we can accept.

A friend is also willing to forgive. "He who covers over an offense promotes love, but whoever repeats the matter separates close friends," instructs Proverbs 17:9. And a friend will not entertain the words of a slanderer, for she knows that "gossip separates close friends" (Proverbs 16:28).

The Bible makes it clear that God is concerned about the way we relate to people. It is crucial that we be in good standing with our friends before we even attempt to draw near to God. Jesus said that if we have a disagreement with someone close to us, we must first be reconciled to that individual before we attempt to worship God (Matthew 5:24).

Clearly, if we want to be women after God's own heart, we must make the cultivation of righteous, encouraging, faith-building friendships a matter of high priority. And in our friendships, let's concentrate on helping each other see the true, honorable, right, pure, lovely, excellent, and praiseworthy qualities of life (Philippians 4:8). We must not allow our coming together with friends to turn into a pity party, but rather make it an uplifting, faith-building session. We must remember that God sees us and is with us. Whenever two or three of us gather together as friends in Christ's name, he is there in our midst (Matthew 18:20).

WHEN FRIENDSHIP CAN'T BE FOUND

Finding a kindred spirit—someone who understands and shares our burdens, interests, and values—is critical for everyone. Commonality enables friends to understand each other, and differences give friends something to exchange with one another. Those who enjoy deep friendships consider their lives enhanced and deepened by these bonds of love. Unfortunately, however, many women do not feel able to participate in a friendship on this deep level.

One young lady recently wrote me a letter describing her struggles. "I struggle with rejection relating back to my childhood," she wrote, "and it affects me in every area of my life. . . . The area that most affects me is in friendships. I don't have a lot to say always and find it hard to converse. Having a low self-image doesn't help. I tend also to look on the negative, not on the positive. . . . I really long to be able to have confidence and have acceptance in life."

Like so many others, this young woman is crying out for a friend who can help her. She is acutely aware of her need for a friend who will stand by her side when she feels unworthy of love. She needs someone who can rescue her from the big black hole of alienation and depression.

My heart goes out to this woman and others who feel inadequate to have or be a friend. Many women struggle with loneliness and are in need of encouragement, acceptance, and love. We all need to know that someone loves us. I know of no better way to start than by developing our relationship with God.

As we grow in understanding and believing that God is our friend—that he loved us so much that he gave his only Son in order that we might be saved—we will see that it is possible to be loved "just because." This is God's uncondi-

tional love. We must embrace, understand, and demonstrate it to others. If you don't feel capable of giving this
kind of love, it's because you really don't "have it in you." It
comes from God, not from you! But our sufficiency is in
Christ. When we are weakest, his strength is able to show
itself in full power!

A friend is someone who understands your past, believes
in your future, and accepts you today just the way you are. If
you have put your faith in Jesus Christ for salvation, you
have such a friend in your Savior. Jesus understands your
past, believes in your future, and accepts you today just the
way you are. He loves you so much that he will stand by you
as you grow in holiness and in his likeness.

When we're filled up with God's love, we are equipped to
reach out to others in friendship. The power of his love
frees us to love others.

FRIENDSHIP WITH GOD

There may come a time in your life when you feel
alone. Perhaps you need to stand strong in an area of righteousness. Everyone around you may think that you are
politically incorrect or out of touch with their "progressive"
reality. Maybe your own family has rejected you because of
your faith in Christ. Perhaps even your husband has cast
you off. But know that you are not alone.

Even if at this time in your life you have no friend to call
on and confide in, there is one to whom you can turn for
all the wonderful counsel, comfort, and wisdom you need.
God has said, "Call to me and I will answer you and tell you
great and unsearchable things you do not know" (Jeremiah
33:3). If we cast our cares upon the Lord, he will sustain us.

I appreciate the words of the old hymn—

What a Friend we have in Jesus,
All our sins and griefs to bear!

> What a privilege to carry
> Everything to God in prayer!

It is indeed an awesome privilege to know the almighty God and enjoy friendship with him.

We can cultivate deep friendships with God, for the Bible tells us that the Lord spoke to Moses face to face, "as a man speaks with his friend" (Exodus 33:11). The Scripture also tells us that Abraham was God's friend (2 Chronicles 20:7), and Job refers to the friendship and counsel of God (Job 29:4). Jesus tells us that we are his friends: "You are my friends if you do what I command. I no longer call you servants, because a servant does not know his master's business. Instead, I have called you friends, for everything that I learned from my Father I have made known to you" (John 15:14-15).

Friendship with God is a two-way street. We cast our burdens on him and commit our ways to him. He, in return, bears our burdens and directs our paths. In faith and gratitude, we obediently follow God's direction. Jesus said that he tells his friends all that his Father has told him; close friends communicate thoroughly and make a transfer of heart and thought.

How awesome is our opportunity to be friends with God, the almighty Creator of all!

QUESTIONS
FOR REFLECTION AND DISCUSSION

1. How does living in an individualist society affect our ability to develop friendships?
2. What role do friends play in our lives?
3. What type of friends should we seek to cultivate?
4. What are the qualities we look for in friends?
5. How have friends made an impact on your life?
6. What can you do to become a better friend?

3

*We Want Respect
and Honor
from Men*

Women want male friends and associates who respect us as
equals and appreciate our contributions, thoughts, accomplishments, and gifts. Men should hold us in high esteem as
equal but distinct creations. Nothing is more irritating than
a man who is convinced that he and his gender are superior
to women. Different we are; but inferior, frail, weak, helpless, and incapable we are not!

As women, we want to be in harmony with our surroundings and to contribute to our society in meaningful and valued ways. If men devalue our accomplishments simply
because they may not be as tangible or lucrative as their
own, this sends the signal that value is measured by money
or fame. Nothing could be farther from the truth, especially for those of us who understand truth as it is revealed
in Scripture. Women are just as vital as men to the success
of the world. And women, like men, need genuine affirmation from time to time.

Whether in the workplace, the community, or the home,
we women want men to respect us *as women,* not as imitation men but in our own right. The distinctions between
men and women should produce mutual benefit and appre-

ciation, not strife or scorn. Men who value women's ideas, insights, and contributions are able to realize the potential for synergy with women.

RESPECT AND COURTESY

Men come into our lives on a regular basis as acquaintances, friends, and coworkers. Men and women are mixed together in our society in a variety of environments. We serve together on committees, we share office space at work, we attend the same parenting consultations, we meet on church boards, and we are even friends. Christian women feel comfortable around men who respect us and conduct themselves in an honorable manner. Christian women want friendships with godly men who are confident in their masculinity and respectful of our femininity.

In my personal conversations with women I have found there is a virtual consensus on the fact that women want their male friends and acquaintances to be gentlemen. According to the *American Heritage Dictionary*, a gentleman is "a polite, gracious, or considerate man with high standards of propriety or correct behavior."

A Christian gentleman is a noble man, one who fulfills God's mandate for his life in caring for and assisting those in his circle of influence. Such a man is always good company for women. He shows courtesy to women in doing simple gestures of consideration, such as opening doors or offering an arm on a slippery sidewalk; and in more significant ways he also shows a deep respect and reverence for women.

Even feminists appreciate kindness, gentleness, and thoughtfulness in men and lament its absence. Feminist Susan Faludi notes that "the share of women in the Roper surveys who agreed that men were 'basically kind, gentle, and thoughtful' fell from 70 percent in 1980 to 50 percent by 1990."[1]

It is not surprising to me that chivalry and benevolence have declined now that some women are telling men they don't need or want men's traditional acts of kindness. Not long ago my husband was entering a college building on a state university campus. As he approached the door he noticed a young coed rushing to enter the building. Because he is a thoughtful gentleman he opened the door for her to enter first, but she stood back and said, "Men don't open doors for me." No wonder men are confused about how to treat women today!

CAN MEN AND WOMEN REALLY BE FRIENDS?

The question has puzzled men and women since the beginning of time, and the answer seems to be both yes and no. There are categories and degrees of friendship. Each person must know his or her own vulnerabilities and work within them.

Looking at the example of Jesus, we see that he enjoyed meaningful friendships with women, including Mary and Martha. No doubt this surprised many people! When Jesus befriended the Samaritan woman at the well, his own disciples "were surprised to find him talking with a woman" (John 4:27). No doubt Jesus wanted to teach his disciples that men and women ought to relate in mutually beneficial ways.

Blaine Smith, noted author and speaker on issues relating to men and women, said to me recently, "If we're cautious and realistic—keeping in mind our ever-present vulnerability—significant friendships can take place between men and women." I agree. Men and women not only *can* be friends, but they *should* be friends.

Nevertheless, the friendships between the sexes will inevitably differ from those within the sexes. Women will relate differently to other women than they do to men. This is both good and normal. In addition, certain precautions must be taken in male/female friendships because of the inherent dangers in them.

The closer a man and woman become in friendship, the greater the tendency for a romantic attachment to develop. This is never desirable in a relationship where marriage is out of the question, and it must be guarded against. The Scriptures, particularly the proverbs of Solomon, overflow with warnings against putting oneself in a sexually tempting situation.

Sexual temptation has occurred, of course, in all societies. It is especially powerful today, now that traditional barriers have been lowered and casual sex is treated by many as a normal part of living.

FREEDOM FROM SEXUAL HARASSMENT

Despite what television commercials and sitcoms, magazine ads, and highway billboards portray, most women do not want to be looked upon by men as sex objects. Scantily clad women in suggestive poses may grab the attention of male consumers and persuade them to buy cigarettes, cars, and alcohol, but they do not represent the image most women would choose for themselves.

And despite what the entertainment industry would lead an unsuspecting public to think, the majority of women are not running after men like starved sex kittens. Certainly such women do exist, but what about the multitude of women who desire healthy, nonsexual friendships and working relationships with men?

One area of increasing concern for many women is that of sexual harassment. Christian women want male friends who are above reproach on every front, including, of course, the sexual arena. Gentlemen do not make sexual remarks or advances. No man but a woman's husband should ever become that intimate with her.

It is not too much to expect a male friend to respect a

woman enough to honor her. A true friend will honor a woman enough not to take advantage of her or act discourteously around her. Gentlemen—good male friends—will refrain from off-color humor and unpleasant language. They will not condescend to women or mock them, and they will not touch women in a way that hints of sexual harassment.

If you have a male friend or associate who does not meet these criteria, perhaps you may need to tell him of your concerns. The information you share could be helpful to him. It's easy to be confused nowadays, and he may have the wrong idea about what women really want. If you are clear about your expectations and he still just doesn't get it, may I suggest that you avoid him.

As Christian friends, men and women are never to do anything that has even the appearance of evil (1 Thessalonians 5:22). When it comes to male/female relationships, we must be vigilant. If an activity might appear to someone else to be evil, we should not engage in it. In Romans 14, Paul wrote that if an activity causes a fellow brother or sister to stumble, we should forego it. Paul even went so far as to say: "It is better not to eat meat or drink wine or to do anything else that will cause your brother to fall" (Romans 14:21). Paul was willing to change his eating habits so that he would not cause a fellow believer to stumble. Indeed, if we walk in love, we will be willing to abstain from a perfectly lawful behavior for the sake of another's conscience.

Today men and women alike are suffering the aftermath of the "freedoms" of the sexual revolution, which has cheapened the God-designed act of sex and lowered the status of women to that of "prey" for hungry, prowling men. It is time to return to the biblical standard of men who relate in purity to women as sisters or mothers or daughters.

We women need to know we can trust the motives and actions of our male friends, acquaintances, and coworkers.

When we are sure we can do this, then we can safely form male/female friendships.

CHARACTERISTICS WE ADMIRE

What are women looking for in our male friends? Here are some character traits on which most of us agree.

Strength. Women like to see backbone in a man. We appreciate male friends who are confident, courageous, and decisive—men who know who they are and what they are called to do in life. Whether or not they are recognized as leaders, their inner strength will spur us on and encourage us.

I find it very unfortunate that the average man today is hesitant and confused about his role in relating to women. The women's movement has misled men into thinking that any act of gentle strength manifested in kindness is an insult to womanhood, and that any show of leadership and protection is an unwanted relic from medieval days. What a pity!

Masculine strength, however, is not to be abused. Some men have embraced the serious misconception that all women are to submit to all men. Nothing could be farther from the truth. Yes, husbands are to lead their wives and male pastors are to lead churches, but no, men are not to lead women! Biblically, women are not commanded to submit to men. In friendships, men and women are to exemplify Christ, challenging each other to grow in the knowledge of Christ and obedience to him. Friends admire each other's strength; one does not consistently instruct or dominate the other.

Godly character. Women want to befriend Christian men whose lives demonstrate godly character and spiritual qualities. John described the stages of Christian maturity when he addressed his epistle to "dear children," "young men," and "fathers" in the faith (1 John 2:12-14).

I believe that where men are today is not as crucial as

where they are headed. Many men have memorized Bible verses, studied the Bible for years, and participated in church activities, but they have never truly surrendered their hearts, lives, and ambitions to God. Others may be young and immature in the faith, but they are committed to the Lord for the long haul. Women enjoy male friends who are not self-absorbed or consumed with appearing super-spiritual, but who are genuine, confident, considerate, and honest as they walk humbly with the Lord.

Christian women desire friendships with men who love the Lord and read his Word. If a man is wholly committed to God, then we can be secure and at ease in his presence.

Humility. Women seek male friends who are humble. "Young men, in the same way be submissive to those who are older," writes Peter. "Clothe yourselves with humility toward one another, because, 'God opposes the proud but gives grace to the humble'" (1 Peter 5:5).

A humble man has no overpowering interest in self-promotion, but is willing to learn through life's circumstances as well as from the people God has put in his life. A humble man will respond to correction with an attitude of submission and openness. He will realize that those whom the Lord loves he reproves (Proverbs 3:12), and that consequently, "the corrections of discipline are the way to life" (Proverbs 6:23).

Integrity. Women desire friendships with men whose lives are characterized by integrity and excellence. The apostle Paul gave a character description of men worthy of being overseers in the church. This description applies to all exemplary Christian men. Paul says they are to be blameless, temperate, sober minded, and not covetous (1 Timothy 3:2-3).

Responsibility. Women desire responsibility and dependability in the friendships they cultivate with men. In our disposable, microwavable, values-poor society, it's not easy to find a trustworthy, reliable friend, male or female. Psalm 15:4 provides a description of a dependable man. He "keeps his oath even when it hurts." In other words, once he has made a commitment, a godly man abides by it, costly as it may be to him.

Irresponsibility in men is rampant in our culture! In the sexual arena, it has led to the ever-growing number of children conceived out of wedlock. Then there is the tragic number of children put to death by their own parents through abortion: 28 million babies have been legally aborted in the United States since 1973.

Irresponsible fathers have been the scourge of our country in recent years. Not even children conceived by married parents are guaranteed a father at home during their childhood since one in two marriages ends in divorce. David Blankenhorn, president of the Institute for American Values, observes that "the experience of fatherlessness is approaching a rough parity with the experience of having a father as an expectation of childhood."[2] Children wounded by divorce often do not get the benefits of child support promised by their irresponsible, runaway fathers. In fact, fatherless children are far more likely than children with fathers to live in poverty.

It is clear that our nation's men are failing to act responsibly. Sadly, men are failing to be there for the children they fathered. Some men never even care to see the children they helped create. An unprecedented number of men are failing to keep the most serious vow of their lives: they are abandoning the women they married. The responsibility that was a common trait in our grandfathers and fathers is rare today.

To be fair, I must add that women are certainly equally at fault for the current sad state of affairs. How often do women have abortions without the father's agreement or knowledge? How often have we failed to fulfill our word

and to do our duty? And how many times have we urged
men to act irresponsibly, to take the easy way out of a difficult situation? Both men and women need to reconsider
responsibility and its importance in a strong society.

Good manners. Women certainly want their male friends
to exercise good manners. If a woman has been taught to
be mannerly, it's particularly grating when others are ill-
mannered. Elisabeth Elliot says:

> Why must I sit up straight, keep elbows off the table
> and napkin in lap? Why does it matter that I eat qui-
> etly and chew with my mouth closed? Why shouldn't I
> talk with my mouth full? Why can't I reach for what I
> want? Why pass the butter to my brother first if I need
> some too? The basic answer is that it makes things
> more pleasant for everybody. "Only a great fool or a
> great genius is likely to flout all social grace with impu-
> nity, and neither one, doing so, makes the most com-
> fortable companion," says Amy Vanderbilt.[3]

Once I was seated at a dinner party where both male and
female friends were present. One man had probably never
been taught manners as a child and showed little knowledge about the basic rules of courtesy. He began to tell a
story during the main course, and he neglected to put his
fork down when he started talking. One forkful of the meal
was already in his mouth, and the second portion was piled
high on his fork waiting to be shoveled in. As his story pro-
ceeded, I found myself not listening to what he was saying,
but noticing that the meat and potatoes in his mouth no
longer looked appetizing. The next forkload, now sus-
pended midway between his plate and his mouth, seemed
in danger of being dumped on the tablecloth. Finally he
paused, loaded the second forkload into his mouth, and

then used his empty but dirty fork to emphasize his gestures as he finished the story.

Believe it or not, he was a very nice man. I cannot remember a thing he said, but I do remember the unusual sight of his food tumbling in his mouth as he spoke. Simple regard for the feelings of the other guests—common courtesy—would have helped him make a much better impression. As Elisabeth Elliot says, "A simple gesture like passing the butter plate to someone else before helping oneself is the outward expression, small and unobtrusive but deeply telling, of the sacrificial principle, 'My life for yours.'"[4]

FALLOUT FROM THE SEXUAL REGRESSION

Women really want male friends who are "pre–sexual revolution" men. We prefer our male friends to treat us with honor and respect as they talk to us as equals, as peers who have intelligence and a quality of life to share.

One of the consequences of the "sexual revolution"—or "sexual regression," as syndicated columnist Joseph Sobran aptly calls it—was the demolition of traditional male and female roles. Certainly some change was called for, but a great deal of the resultant overhaul was not. The noble pursuit of equality has been distorted into a quest for role interchangeability. John Piper makes some interesting observations about male/female roles as they exist today:

> The tendency today is to stress the equality of men and women by minimizing the unique significance of our maleness or femaleness. But this depreciation of male and female personhood is a great loss. It is taking a tremendous toll on generations of young men and women who do not know what it means to be a man or a woman. Confusion over the meaning of sexual personhood today is epidemic. The consequence of this confusion is not a free and happy harmony among

gender-free persons relating on the basis of abstract competencies. The consequence rather is more divorce, more homosexuality, more sexual abuse, more promiscuity, more social awkwardness, and more emotional distress and suicide that comes with the loss of God-given identity.[5]

More than once I have wished that we could delete the sexual regression from our history. The rebellion of the sixties—brought about largely by feminists—lambasted the noble notion of a gentleman, leaving men uncertain about their roles as men in relation to women, and leaving women equally confused about their own identity. In addition, women have been sorely disappointed in the new, irresponsible, commitment-phobic man produced by the sexual revolution. For years feminists have claimed that what women want from men is sexual "freedom" and financial independence. To the detriment of all and the regret of the majority of women, the feminist objectives in the area of sexual "freedom" have been largely realized.

As a direct result of this so-called sexual freedom, women today are more encumbered and burdened than ever before. Most single mothers will agree that the loneliness and pain sexual "freedom" brings is nothing short of devastating. Statistics show that in addition to the emotional poverty it generates, single motherhood—a natural consequence of sexual freedom—is an extremely accurate predictor of material poverty. (Single-parent families are nearly six times more likely to be poor than two-parent families.) Since financial security is usually a significant contributor to a person's well-being, it amazes me that "progressive" thinkers don't recognize that the so-called sexual freedom came with an awfully steep price tag.

Has it taken a generation of sexual regression for us to discover that men and women relate best to each other when following the Master's plan that gives sex its rightful place in monogamous marriage? Wouldn't much of the pain, heartache, and destruction have been avoided if we had simply obeyed the principles in God's Word? The answer is a resounding *yes!* Without a doubt, God always knows best.

Interestingly, much of what the Bible has to say about the relationships of men and women actually finds support in modern scientific findings on the distinctions between women and men.

UNDERSTANDING MALE/FEMALE DIFFERENCES

Men and women are different. This fact should be obvious to all, but as we know, some women feel a need to minimize and even deny such differences. God made Adam one way and Eve another. Their differences were intended for the completion of men and women, not for competition between us. It is important to women that our male friends understand and acknowledge the differences that exist between us. After all, distinctions do not mean that one sex is superior to the other. They simply indicate that we have different roles, gifts, and effects.

Much secular science corroborates the idea that there are significant differences between the genders on many fronts. Anne Moir, author of a recent book on the differences in men's and women's brain structure, emphasizes the importance of these dissimilarities: "Men are different from women. To maintain that they are the same in aptitude, skill or behavior is to build a society based on a biological and scientific lie."[6] Moir writes that male and female brains are structurally different even before birth. Acting in tandem with hormones, they produce different perceptions, priorities, and behavior.

Most women, for instance, are more multifaceted in their thinking, while men are more singly focused. Women have

more gray matter, which facilitates organizing and process-
ing information in the brain. In women, the mass of fibers
connecting the brain's two hemispheres, the *corpus callosum,*
is larger in proportion to brain weight than that of men.
This is believed to promote greater communication between the two hemispheres of the brain.

What is commonly known as "women's intuition" is no
doubt a result of the different makeup of our brains.
Women tend to see problems from all sides and read facial
and body language to a greater degree than do men. Men
tend to be more "one-dimensional" in thinking; they may
be blind to what women would consider obvious.

The different makeup of the male brain complements
the female's way of thinking. Men have more white matter,
which facilitates sending information and benefits motor
coordination.

Men are generally better than women at visual tasks,
maps, mazes, three-dimensional rotation, and sense of direction. They are also typically better at spatial games. One
study found that "females depend more on landmarks to
navigate, while males use a system of vectors—calculating
how far and in what direction they travel."[7]

It has been observed that men think in a more linear way
than do women. They "see A and B and arrive at C," says
Moir. "They are not distracted."[8] Women, by contrast, tend
to gather information not only from A and B but also from
D and E and even Q before arriving at C.

As time goes on, more and more research shows that the
two sexes are intricately complementary. Our Creator knew
what he was doing.

In addition to the different ways we perceive and interpret our environment, men and women differ in communication styles. Women tend to talk more than men. Men
generally talk only to give or get information, whereas
women talk for that reason as well as for the purpose of

exploring and developing thoughts, releasing stress, and creating intimacy.[9] Have you ever noticed that when two men are having a friendly conversation, they often stand side by side, but when two women talk, they stand directly in front of each other? Women use verbal communication and body language to bond with each other, whereas men use verbal communication primarily to process information.

Deborah Tannen, author of *You Just Don't Understand: Men and Women in Conversation,* found that men turn conversations into competitions for power. Women, by contrast, tend to view conversations as negotiations for closeness in which people seek and give confirmation and support and try to reach consensus.[10] Perhaps it is our need for intimacy and affirmation that has strengthened our communication skills.

WHY DENY THE DIFFERENCES?

Some feminists try to avoid discussion of the very real physical, psychological, and social differences between men and women, because these distinctions don't do much to support their ideology. Tannen observes that "the desire to affirm that women are equal has made some scholars reluctant to show they are different, because differences can be used to justify unequal treatment and opportunity."[11]

It is interesting to note that in spite of the negative impact these findings may have on feminist ideology, Tannen feels compelled to reveal them. She realizes that understanding and honoring the differences between men and women plays a pivotal role in forming and maintaining healthy relationships between the sexes:

> Denying real differences can only compound the confusion that is already widespread in this area of shifting and reforming relationships between men and women.
> Pretending that women and men are the same hurts women, because the ways they are treated are based on

the norms for men. It also hurts men who, with good intentions, speak to women as they would to men, and are nonplussed when their words don't work as they expected, or even spark resentment and anger.[12]

It is clear that in spite of feminist rhetoric downplaying the uniqueness of men and women, there's no denying the fundamental differences between us. Woman, of course, is the only sex capable of giving birth to and nursing a child. Our unique brain structure produces subtle and not-so-subtle differences in the way we interpret our surroundings. Our conversational style differs from that of men. When it comes to relationships—the crux of life—men and women have different needs and experiences.

Unless women become tough and callous, repressing our God-given sensitive nature, we will always be hurt when treated roughly. We are not "one of the boys." We are women, and we want men's appreciation for who we are.

I'm not saying men should treat us as though we are weak, powerless, incapable, inferior creatures. Far from it—we've all seen the power of a determined woman! We want men to encourage us to exercise our influence in a godly way. We want the power to be meek, not weak. This power will free us to live according to our feminine nature as nurturers, supporters, and bearers of culture and civility.

We would like men to understand us as women and to stop competing against us as if we were imitation men. We would like them to befriend, defend, and support us. We would like both men and women to be free to be the friends God designed us to be.

BIBLICAL MASCULINITY

The chaos created by confusion over the roles of men and women inspired John Piper and Wayne Grudem to compile and edit a series of articles on this volatile topic. In their book *Recovering Biblical Manhood & Womanhood,* the contributors clearly and succinctly define men's and women's roles from a biblical perspective. Using the Scriptures as a plumb line, the authors peel away cultural, time-sensitive biases and demonstrate the extent to which feminist ideology has infiltrated Christian thinking. The timeless biblical model of masculinity and femininity these theologians present is worthy of serious consideration.

"At the heart of mature masculinity," write Piper and Grudem, "is a sense of benevolent responsibility to lead, provide for and protect women in ways appropriate to a man's differing relationships."[13] "Mature masculinity" means that "a man's sense of responsibility is in the process of growing out of its sinful distortions and limitations, and finding its true nature as a form of love, not a form of self-assertion."[14] "The aim of leadership," writes John Piper, "is not to demonstrate the superiority of the leader, but to bring out all the strengths of people that will move them forward to the desired goal."[15]

Biblical leadership involves being the servant of all: "You know that the rulers of the Gentiles lord it over them, and their high officials exercise authority over them," Jesus told his disciples. "Not so with you. Instead, whoever wants to become great among you must be your servant, and whoever wants to be first must be your slave—just as the Son of Man did not come to be served, but to serve, and to give his life as a ransom for many" (Matthew 20:25-28).

A man will feel an instinctive desire to protect his female friends and to assist them in things they might not normally enjoy doing, be it changing a tire or helping move a heavy load. I cannot believe that any woman, deep down, would not appreciate the protective instinct of a man who walks her to her car in the evening, making sure she has a safe start home. Some might falsely call this chauvinism; I call it courtesy and concern.

Piper continues his definition of biblical masculinity by describing the term *benevolent* in this context:

> This word is intended to show that the responsibility of manhood is for the good of woman. Benevolent responsibility is meant to rule out all self-aggrandizing authoritarianism (cf. Luke 22:26). It is meant to rule out all disdaining condescension and any act that makes a mature woman feel patronized rather than honored and prized (cf. 1 Peter 3:7). The word "benevolent" is meant to signal that mature masculinity gives appropriate expression to the Golden Rule in male-female relationships (Matthew 7:12).[16]

If more men were to live according to God's design, there would be no market for feminist ideology. Women would be inspired to encourage men, even as men would encourage us by their lives! Men and women would be friends, not adversaries. Women would feel secure and fulfilled living according to the Creator's design. "At the heart of mature femininity," write Piper and Grudem, "is a freeing disposition to affirm, receive, and nurture strength and leadership from worthy men in ways appropriate to a woman's differing relationships."[17]

Women have an inborn desire to affirm and nurture others. It is hard to affirm those who mistreat and dishonor us, but those who accept and enjoy us as equals will surely receive the benefits of the nature God gave us. They will receive our affirmation, encouragement, and support. Men need women, and women need men. Feminism spurns this notion and rejects the idea of men showing kindness and respect to women because of their gender. Consequently, women who would like to consider themselves progressive are torn between the feminist dictates and the innate desire for courtesy.

Men who understand and embrace their God-given identity are those who will proceed securely in life. Such men will enjoy rather than undermine the distinctions between themselves and others, men and women alike. In the presence of such men, women will feel secure, accepted, enjoyed, and at peace.

Women desire male friends and associates who are confidently living out their manhood as God designed, and who therefore are unafraid to show respect and honor to women.

QUESTIONS
FOR REFLECTION AND DISCUSSION

1. What precautions can a man and woman take to avoid the dangers of sexual temptation that frequently accompany intimate friendships?
2. How would you describe the modern-day gentleman?
3. How has the "sexual revolution" affected the roles of men and women?
4. What are some of the ways in which men and women differ?
5. What character qualities do we look for in male friends?
6. How can women develop healthy nonphysical friendships with men?
7. How can men and women relate in mutually beneficial ways?

4

We Want
Purpose and
Examples

*O*ur *lives are littered with mid-course corrections. A full half of us divorced. Many of the women have had career paths that look like games of Chutes and Ladders. We have changed directions and priorities again and again. But our "mistakes" become crucial parts, sometimes the best parts, of the lives we have made.*

Ellen Goodman[1]

I don't know about you, but I'd think there was a serious problem with my personal philosophy if it led me to divorce, change priorities time after time, and follow a topsy-turvy career path. But, sadly enough, women who follow the ideals of feminism find themselves just as Ellen Goodman describes, with their lives "littered" and broken.

Caught in the middle of a feminist/traditionalist battleground, today's women face two options: Should we join forces with the feminist agitators who would destroy the "patriarchal" system so we can spend our lives in self-direction, or should we join those who are working to preserve the traditional family so we can be part of something greater than ourselves? Whose lives can we look to as models and guides?

RESTLESS WOMEN IN SEARCH OF A PURPOSE

Feminist Judith Bardwick observes that our culture is undergoing such rapid changes in basic values and beliefs that our society has become unstable. "Many have been and will continue to be forced, by changes in their values or changes in the values of others, to significantly alter how they behave," she says. "Shifts in basic values have created profound dislocations for the large number of people whose lives have become very different from what they expected when they were growing up."[2]

Restless women who have not yet found the purpose for their lives have borne the brunt of society's instability. Like the women described by Ellen Goodman, they have impermanent families, shifting priorities, and a "do your own thing" philosophy. The attacks on traditional Christian morality have afflicted many women with an uneasiness about their purpose and role.

All of us are in transition, but where are we going? The feminist movement, Bardwick writes, "is clearest about what it is rejecting from the past. But the movement is not clear about what norms will replace those which have been rejected; new norms are hard to imagine."[3]

In other words, feminists don't like where we've been, but they have no idea where we're headed! That is a frightening thought. They are bent on destroying traditional morality and restructuring our society, but they aren't sure if their new order will work.

Look at the impact of feminism in just one minor area: expressions of courtesy. Two of the original "Christian feminists," Letha Scanzoni and Nancy Hardesty, predicted nearly twenty years ago what has become reality today:

> The end of male chauvinism will also mean the end of chivalry in the traditional sense of men continually smoothing the way for the 'weaker sex.' Women can

no longer expect doors to open, seats to become
vacant, packages to be carried for them simply because
they're women. . . . But hopefully, courtesy and consideration will be extended to all persons on an equal
basis.[4]

Did women really want to be treated like men? Did we
want to lose the respect and honor once shown to us? Did
we want to lose romance? I, for one, did not and do not. I
still enjoy doors being opened for me and seats being
offered to me, not because I am frail and unable to do
things for myself, but because those are gestures of respect
and dignity offered to the feminine woman. I don't feel
demeaned or less than human when a gentlemen openly
shows his respect for me. Yet all of this is being lost as feminists strive to build their vision of utopia.

We will lose far more than chivalry if feminists achieve
their goals. We will lose love, compassion, gentleness, and
warmth in all of our relationships. These have already been
lost in many male/female relationships where lust has been
substituted for love. Perhaps we are seeing increased allega-
tions of sexual harassment today because feminist admoni-
tions have stripped women of the respect and dignity
traditionally given to them.

To insist that women be treated "equally" with men—that
is, if by *equally with* we mean *identically to*—not only injures
women, but it deprives men of a natural need to protect
and support. It creates insecurities, fear, and confusion.
Men no longer know how to treat women. They're not sure
what women expect or what will insult us. Instead of bringing us together, "equal treatment" creates a gap between us
as we compete with each other. The relationship between
men and women should be one of cooperation, not fierce
competition.

As they compete in the work force, many women become

masculine in their appearance and manner. Few men are attracted to a macho-feminist. A masculine man is attracted by feminine characteristics in a woman. He's not seeking a clone of himself, but a complementary being with traits that he lacks but desires. Similarly, women are attracted to men with attributes they lack but admire. Within the marriage bond, a man and woman find completeness. They will become one.

Unfortunately, many women don't realize the truth of the old axiom "opposites attract," and they reject their natural feminine nature in favor of masculinity. Even Judith Bardwick is worried about the ultimate feminist goal of an androgynous (unisex) society where all sexual distinctions have been erased:

> The danger of the androgynous vision lies in the possibility that our goal will become the development of an asexual culture. While many of the things that we do are essentially asexual in the sense that it does not make any difference whether they are done by a woman or a man, it would be a pity if an emphasis on androgyny blurred the complementary excitements that are created from the differences in how women and men perceive and feel.[5]

A TIME TO RECONSIDER

From all indications, women today from both within and without the feminist movement are finally coming to grips with the reality of human nature. They want more than careers and equality. They don't want the "best parts" of their lives to be divorces and career changes and broken hearts. They want an eternal purpose and meaning for life itself.

As some feminist activists pass thirty or even forty years of age, they find themselves agonizing over whether or not they should have babies. As my husband, Tim, mentions in his book *The Battle for the Family,* hard-line feminist Phyllis Chesler finally felt she needed to have a child, even though she had no husband. She knew she was going to be rebuffed by her allies in the feminist movement when she said, "The unique intimacy and transcendence offered in the birth of a child was something I didn't want to deny myself."[6]

Indeed, many feminists see child rearing as a grand cop-out. "It is easier to live through someone else than to become complete yourself," Betty Friedan wrote in *The Feminine Mystique.*[7] But in spite of the feminist aversion to child rearing, many women are realizing that it might not be a bad idea to get married to a loving husband, have and rear children, and live a peaceful life in suburbia. These women have finally seen where the women's movement is leading them—toward a life of emptiness, anger, and loneliness.

An increasing number of women are taking time to re-evaluate the direction of the feminist/humanist philosophy. They are either losing interest in it or making a deliberate turn in their attitudes regarding family, God, and country. The feminist leaders do not represent the majority of American women today.

Not long ago, a former feminist met me after a speaking engagement and related how her whole life had been spent fighting for the Equal Rights Amendment. She had marched in demonstrations and been active in the National Organization for Women, but her eyes were opened to the harm the ERA would cause her family. Today she has committed herself to wholeheartedly supporting pro-family causes.

I recently received a letter from a woman who had been influenced by the women's movement. As she recounted the sad story of her life, she told me how she had voted for the radical Peace and Freedom party, picketed with feminists, and smoked marijuana—all in the name of liberation. She recounted that many of the feminists she met were lesbians, atheists, and antifamily. As she tried to become a liberated female she became "alienated, not liberated." As a result of following the feminist ideals of "womanhood," this woman developed a serious drinking problem, deserted her husband, and had several abortions. Today, as a consequence of her sexual "freedom," she is sterile.

Fortunately, this woman's story did not end with this string of personal tragedies. In her desperation she sought the Lord for help, and he heard her prayers! She told me that she's now a committed Christian who is absolutely opposed to the goals of the feminist movement. She has found a new purpose for her life.

CREATED FOR OTHERS, NOT SELF

Many in the women's movement would say they live and work for "liberation," but true liberation is not found by leaving behind those we love. Only by living according to God's Word can a woman become truly liberated. Unfortunately, many women have been deceived and made captives of godless philosophies. In this regard, Paul has a stern warning for us: "See to it that no one takes you captive through hollow and deceptive philosophy, which depends on human tradition and the basic principles of this world rather than on Christ" (Colossians 2:8).

As a result of the deception under which they labor, feminists are often miserable, angry people. The only possible way they will ever find contentment is to turn from their vain, godless philosophies and embrace the Son of God. Only then will they have true peace and freedom.

The basic difference between a restless woman and a woman who is committed to Christ is *why* she lives. A thread of selfishness runs through all feminist writings. There is an emphasis on *my* rights, *my* goals, *my* body, and *my* self-fulfillment. Feminists have openly admitted that the invention of the birth-control pill and the legalization of abortion have been powerful social forces in radicalizing women. The "freedom" to fornicate outside marriage and to murder unborn children is looked upon as a great stride forward in the status of women.

Feminism, then, exists simply for self-advancement. This trend toward selfishness is, however, self-destructive rather than liberating. Albert Einstein, genius that he was, knew the futility of selfishness. "Only a life lived for others," he said, "is the life worth while."[8]

Selfishness goes against what I believe is the basic nature of a woman to care for others. Some feminist psychologists look on *selflessness* as a neurotic behavior instilled in women by a male-oriented social system. But I believe God gave women a natural tendency toward giving, nurturing, serving, and comforting. To deny this selfless nature is to deny our personalities and the purpose for our existence.

Throughout the Bible we are taught to be more concerned for others than for ourselves. Through acts of giving we find fulfillment and purpose. In Philippians 2:3-8 God tells us,

> Do nothing out of selfish ambition or vain conceit, but in humility consider others better than yourselves. Each of you should look not only to your own interests, but also to the interests of others. Your attitude should be the same as that of Christ Jesus: Who, being in very nature God, did not consider equality with God something to be grasped, but made himself nothing, taking the very nature of a servant, being made in human likeness. And being found in appearance as a man, he humbled himself and became obedient to death—even death on a cross!

Whether we are male or female, our purpose in life is to be concerned with two goals: loving God and loving others. It is not a sin to take care of our own needs, but we should be willing to give of ourselves to others. Our attitude should be one of humility, not rebellion.

THE NEW TRADITIONAL ACTIVISTS

In his book *Back to Basics,* Burton Yale Pines notes the growing traditionalist movement:

> No longer does the feminist movement by itself set the agenda for debate on women's issues. No longer is this movement the voice which policy-makers hear speaking for all American women. Shattering this onetime feminist monopoly are women who previously were content to remain in their kitchens and care for their families and who defined "activism" as attending PTA meetings and baking for church bazaars.[9]

Political analyst, writer, and homemaker, Connaught Marshner has given a name to this new kind of leader who has come out of the kitchen to speak for American women. She is the "new traditional woman," and she realizes that certain moral principles and social institutions must be preserved if we are to have any kind of orderly, civilized society. This woman realizes that God has created male and female and has given us clear instructions on how we are to treat one another. We do not have to flounder with situational ethics or be confused about right and wrong.

The new traditional woman, Marshner says,

> will transmit civilization and humanity to the twenty-first century. Make no mistake. It is women who will do it. This involves nothing less than a change of heart by a whole generation. To save our society, we must

change our hearts, and change the hearts of our fellow men. If our hearts are changed, our politics will
change, and our public policies will change.[10]

Depending upon the choices we make, we can change
our society for better or for worse. I believe all of us—
whether restless or content, churched or unchurched—
have choices to make about our lives' priorities. And when
we discover the eternal purpose for our lives, all of our
choices and priorities will reflect that purpose.

Jesus came into the world, not to rule over us, but to
serve us and redeem us from the curse of sin. Jesus should
be our model and guide. At one point in his ministry he
washed his disciples' feet to show that they should have the
same humility in serving others. If the God of creation was
willing to wash feet, shouldn't we be willing to serve others?

How different Jesus' attitude is from that of the world.
The world teaches us to fight for our rights; we must strive
and claw our way to the top. We must picket, protest,
scream, and destroy so we can have our own way. But what
is the fruit of the world's way? Littered lives and broken
hearts. Look around at your friends and relatives, and
doubtless you will see the fruit of the world's philosophy
there. All of us know someone who has been severely hurt
by selfishness.

We women have two choices: one is to accept the nebulous goals of the world's women; the other is to accept
God's wisdom and his purpose for our lives. The apostle
James outlined our choices in James 3:16-17: "For where
you have envy and selfish ambition, there you find disorder
and every evil practice. But the wisdom that comes from
heaven is first of all pure; then peace-loving, considerate,
submissive, full of mercy and good fruit, impartial and sincere."

Worldly goals, based upon selfish ambition and rebellion,

lead nowhere. A life spent in pursuit of selfish goals is empty, with no ultimate direction or purpose. But a life spent in service to God and others leads to peace and joy.

Evaluate your own direction. What is your purpose in life?

FINDING GODLY EXAMPLES

Today's woman, caught between feminist theories and Christian ideals, often doesn't know where to turn. The feminists tell her she needs to "update" her thinking, eliminate gender distinctions, and be suspicious of men. The Christian message, in stark contrast, tells her to prize her womanhood, embrace her God-given identity, and, if she is married, submit to her husband.

While the feminist agenda evolves, the Christian message remains steadfast. Because it is based on objective, eternal truth, it is able to withstand the storms of opposing public opinion. When we believe in Christ, we are able to have such firm faith, and we must confidently live by it and defend it in the face of adversity.

Yet too many of us are ignorant of what we believe and why. We are easily intimidated and overwhelmed by women who may have studied more than we, or whose professional attainments exceed ours. This ought not to be. Hesitation and doubt are our downfall. We must be strong in the Lord. You and I need to become familiar and adept with our spiritual and ideological weapons in order to win the battle.

To this end, we women need heroines. We want to see living examples of Christian women who stand against the tide of immoral, godless, feminist teaching.

But how can we find Christian heroines when at times it seems that our country has completely forsaken its godly heritage? While it is true that the United States is suffering terrible ills as a result of sin on many fronts, there are pockets of spiritual growth and health. According to a recent Gallup poll, 94 percent of Americans "believe in God or some kind of unseen spirit," and 84 percent of Americans view God as the "heavenly Father of the Bible who can be reached by prayers."[11] Women are apparently more spiritually inclined than are men. For instance, the Gallup polls show that while 91 percent of women pray, only 85 percent of men do.

Like salt sprinkled throughout meat that would otherwise decay and be lost, Christians are preserving our country. Yes, our nation is suffering from sin. Yes, feminists and others have made dangerous inroads into the well-being of our society. Yes, homosexuals have gained political acceptance to a great degree. And yes, abortion is being tolerated and even supported by those who traditionally opposed it. But let's not forget that though we are in a battle, we are destined to win. We have built on the moral foundation of our forefathers, and we are a mighty army of women armed with the power of prayer.

AN ARMY OF HEROINES

As Bible-believing women, we are a formidable force, whether the media recognizes us or not. You may have noticed that the media view of women tends to highlight the armies of feminists marching for their rights instead of the armies of women who volunteer at nursing homes, the Red Cross, crisis pregnancy centers, and schools across the country. You won't see women missionaries working among primitive tribes on an installment of " $^{20}/_{20}$. " But mission hospitals, orphanages, and schools around the world are heavily staffed with caring Christian women. Maternity homes and crisis pregnancy centers throughout our country are kept going by volunteer women who faithfully give of themselves to help others.

Just as the press does not acknowledge women who are spending their lives to help others in need, so it generally ignores the story of the politically active, conservative women who are working to preserve the American family. But we can't let this fact discourage us. Instead, we realize our fight is against an unseen enemy, against spiritual forces of wickedness in high places. And though our enemy is invisible and immaterial, the results of our prayers and participation in this heavenly battle can be seen and touched. We have seen lives encouraged, healed, protected, and saved.

Godly women have filled an important role in American history. The number of women actively involved in church work has always outnumbered men. A study of women and religion in America showed that

> female church members had vastly outnumbered males during most of the colonial period. Even during revivals, which were particularly effective in recruiting male converts, men had not always equaled the number of women joining. During the First Great Awakening (1739–1743), for example, the proportion of women admitted to Connecticut churches averaged about 56 percent.[12]

Women took leadership roles in organizing missionary societies to share the gospel overseas. According to historian Rosemary Skinner Keller, "More females became involved in women's missionary society work after the Civil War than in all areas of the social reform and women's rights movements combined. Between 1861 and 1894, foreign missionary societies were organized by and for women in thirty-three denominations, and home missionary societies in seventeen."[13] Women concerned for the spiritual welfare of others have made an eternal difference in the lives of many.

Let's look at Frances Willard and Catherine Beecher, two women who helped pave the way for our good and prosperity. You won't find their stories in your newspaper or featured in a television documentary, but I'm delighted to share them with you.

FRANCES WILLARD AND FAMILY PRESERVATION

In the nineteenth century, alcoholism, urban poverty, and child abuse were major problems in every American city. Something needed desperately to be done, and one brave women stepped up to meet the need.

Frances Willard stood alone as the moving force behind the Women's Christian Temperance Union, originally formed to attack the problem of alcohol abuse. When Miss Willard was elected president of the WCTU in 1879, she broadened the concerns of the organization beyond alcoholism to other social problems. Under her brilliant leadership the WCTU crusaded for women's suffrage, better schools, labor reform, prison reform, urban welfare, help for prostitutes, and an end to the use of narcotics.[14]

Miss Willard understood the vital link between Christian beliefs and action. Her strong Christian convictions were translated into specific reforms aimed at uplifting the lot of mankind, not only in the United States, but around the world.

Miss Willard's major concern was to preserve the American family. All the social problems she dealt with threatened the safety of the home in one way or another. She was determined to protect and defend the institution of marriage from outside forces.

In her autobiography, Miss Willard wrote:

> With all its faults, and they are many, I believe the present marriage system to be the greatest triumph of Christianity, in that it has created and conserves more happy homes than the world has ever known. Any law that renders less binding the mutual, life-long loyalty

of one man and one woman to each other, which is
the central idea of every home, is an unmitigated
curse to that man and woman, to that home, and to
humanity.[15]

Frances Willard did not spend a lifetime demanding her
"rights." She was not motivated by hatred, but by compassion. She saw men and women suffering the effects of alcohol and drug abuse, prostitution, and oppression. She
determined to use all the power at her disposal to rectify
the injustices she saw in society. Her motives were not selfish. They were directed toward bettering the lives of all men
and women.

CATHERINE BEECHER AND CHARACTER DEVELOPMENT

Another zealous Christian woman of the nineteenth
century was Catherine Beecher, who spent her life crusading for educational reforms. She established training insti-
tutes to educate young women in homemaking and the
arts, believing that women had a special role to fulfill as
mothers and wives.

By educating young women in the science of what later
came to be known as "home economics," Catherine
Beecher felt they would be greater assets to their husbands
and children. In her view, God gave women the responsibility of training children in righteousness. (Her view was only
partially correct: The Bible teaches that both the father and
mother are to train up their children.) Through her volumi-
nous writings Catherine Beecher became the most famous
spokeswoman for the "traditionalist" cause during the nineteenth century.

Toward the end of the nineteenth century, editors of
women's magazines joined women reformers and churches
in pressing for needed reforms. According to political com-

mentator Reo M. Christenson, about one-third of the articles in *Ladies' Home Journal, The Women's Home Companion,* and *Good Housekeeping* from 1890 to 1910 dealt with the importance of child rearing, character development, and the mother's character in modeling the future leaders of the nation.

At the turn of the century, Edward Bok was editor of *The Ladies' Home Journal.* Bok also served as an editor of a unique ten-volume set of inspirational books designed for children and young adults. *The Library of Inspiration and Achievement* was filled with articles promoting morality, honesty, thrift, and heroism. Its purpose was to instill sound Christian principles in youth.

In one essay Bok told his young readers:

> There is no influence to be compared with that of a good woman over the life of a young man. It means everything to him, his success in every phase of life. Men are by nature coarse and brutal; it is the influence of woman which softens them. But no influence is productive of the best and surest results unless we make ourselves susceptible to it. If we lack faith in women, if we fail in the right ideal of womanhood, all her influence will be as naught upon us. . . . Man's best friend is the woman who loves him. That should be the faith of every young man toward woman; that should be his absolute conviction, and he should show it by an attitude of respect and deference toward her.[16]

Because of the character education promoted in books, women's magazines, and the popular *McGuffey's Reader,* America's crime rate actually declined for a whole century. Only during the 1920s—an age of rebellion—did the crime rate begin to rise again. Women of the nineteenth century had a tremendously civilizing effect on their society, and women today can also change the world we live in. The moral climate of our world depends greatly on the stature of its women.

HEROINES FOR TODAY

Heroic Christian women are not "trapped house-wives," but intelligent, dedicated, and hardworking leaders. Heroic women are exemplified by the virtuous woman described in the thirty-first chapter of Proverbs. They are keepers of the home as well as active in their community. They are like the wise woman described in Proverbs 14:1: "The wise woman builds her house, but with her own hands the foolish one tears hers down."

Heroic women know their purpose in life is not to satisfy their own desires, but to minister healing, love, and hope to the less fortunate. They are selflessly devoted to their partic-ular cause, whether it is pulling young women out of prosti-tution, saving the lives of unborn children, or crusading against alcohol and drug abuse. They are not devoting their lives to the elusive goal of "self-fulfillment," because they are fulfilled and happy as a result of their willingness to give of themselves.

Hundreds of thousands of women today are involved in organizations such as Concerned Women for America, Christian Action Council, Eagle Forum, American Life League, Enough Is Enough, and Mothers Against Drunk Driving, to name just a few. These women know who they are. They are confident of their worth; they see the decline in American society, and they are actively involved in trying to stop it.

The committed women of Concerned Women for Amer-ica, for instance, are working in churches and neighbor-hoods to build a network of prayer and action. They are actively working at the local, state, and national levels to derail legislation and education that will harm their families. They are concerned about protecting the rights of families rather than their own personal rights. They are not primarily concerned about self-fulfillment, and they are not chasing some nebulous ideal of happiness. They are seeking to fill a concrete need: preserving the nuclear family and society from destruction.

A statesman from Israel once told my dear friend Mary Crowley that "no nation, no culture, and no society can rise above the standards of their women."

Women can be heroes! I believe that what we need today are biblical role models—women who are living their everyday lives according to the principles of Scripture. Biblical heroines need not be intimidated by the intellectual class that arrogantly parades itself as the judge and final arbiter over the Word of God. Biblical heroines are everyday women like you and me who dare to step out in faith and obedience to God's commands.

Each woman's call is unique. For some, obedience to God means being "thrown to the lions," so to speak, or cast into a hostile climate in which Christians and the Bible are scorned as out of date and puritanical. For others, obedience to God may lead to a more quiet, private existence. The important thing, however, is to be obedient to God and "stand firm. Let nothing move you. Always give yourselves fully to the work of the Lord, because you know that your labor in the Lord is not in vain" (1 Corinthians 15:58).

Wherever God's call leads you, keep in mind that in God's eyes, the true heroes and heroines are those who remain steadfast, immovable, and unshaken in obedience to him, even when facing fiercely contrary winds.

QUESTIONS
FOR REFLECTION AND DISCUSSION

1. What is a woman's basic God-given nature?
2. Why is it important to have godly role models?
3. Who are your contemporary role models?
4. What type of women are heroines in God's eyes?
5. How can women make history for God today?
6. In what ways do women serve as society's civilizers?

DESIRES IN OUR FAMILY LIFE

5

We Want to Be Fulfilled Single Women

A prominent newspaper recently featured an article titled "Divorced, Middle-Aged and Happy: Women, Especially, Adjust to the 90s." I was curious to read the article because my husband and I have ministered to many newly single women who had divorced, and few of them called themselves happy. The article stated that women are "learning to be self-sufficient and they are choosing singleness rather than losing their independence."[1]

I don't believe everything I read in the paper, and I'm sure you don't either. I think most of us recognize that most women do not dream of years of singleness and independence. Whatever feminists may tell the world, most women still treasure the concept of marriage. The idea of growing old alone is not a very pleasant thought. There are many aging senior citizens who are lonely and would give anything to have a companion at this stage of their lives.

Still, the number of single women is growing rapidly. According to a March 1991 Census Bureau report, only 90 percent of Americans will ever get married, compared to the historical rate of 95 percent. For those who do marry, statistics indicate that at least four out of ten first marriages will end in divorce.

Singleness is widespread in our society for many reasons. Divorced parents are often reluctant to marry again and risk the pain of still another divorce. The lure of romantic love is no longer a compelling incentive for marriage, because society freely condones couples living together outside of marriage. "Why marry when I can enjoy the benefits of married life without its responsibilities?" many people reason. Obviously, those who say such things have no idea of the profound bonding and deep love that is reserved for marriage. There is much more to marriage than the sexual relationship.

Some women have postponed marriage because they have swallowed the feminists' line that women must "find" and "be" themselves apart from male intervention. Generally speaking, however, single women do not accept this view. Far from it, most are willing and available for marriage, but for one reason or another have not had the right opportunity for marriage. The search for Prince Charming can take women along a long, winding path.

Another category of women who have not married are those who have chosen celibacy as a way of life. Paul writes favorably about the gift of celibacy, noting that "an unmarried woman or virgin is concerned about the Lord's affairs: Her aim is to be devoted to the Lord in both body and spirit. But a married woman is concerned about the affairs of this world—how she can please her husband" (1 Corinthians 7:34). Those who are unmarried are free from the inevitable distractions associated with marriage and are thus free to serve the Lord unhindered. Those who have the gift of celibacy should consider themselves singularly blessed!

SEXUALLY ACTIVE CHRISTIAN SINGLES?

Unmarried, celibate women can find peace in living a pure life-style, but a surprisingly large number of people who refer to themselves as "Christian singles" are living according to the world's standards. In a national broadcast by Focus on the Family, the speaker stated that probably 50 percent of people who call themselves Christian singles are "sexually active" (a euphemism for "sexually immoral").[2] This is a shameful statistic. We aren't surprised when non-Christian singles live by immoral standards, but Christians should have a different set of rules to live by. Our standards are based on the Word of God, and the Christian church is in desperate need of a wake-up call on this issue.

Sexual sin is a dead-end street leading to destruction, low self-esteem, disappointment, hurt, and emotional scarring (not to mention the possible physical diseases, including AIDS). The attempt to find happiness in fulfilling fleeting lusts has never left a person satisfied, nor will it. The book of Proverbs is filled with warnings against indulging in immorality.

Please understand: I recognize that it's not easy to maintain moral purity in a morally depraved generation. It may be particularly difficult for singles who have passed the age by which they had always expected to be married and are surrounded by a culture that flouts traditional sexual morality.

Making the task harder yet is the typical single woman's desire for intimacy. She desires to be the confidante of a godly man and craves the emotional and physical oneness of the marital relationship. She finds it difficult to find her place in a world created for couples. How is she to deal with the sexual temptations that may plague her? And where should she "draw the line" with regard to a physical relationship?

A godly single woman does not expect to end up under the sheets with a man just because she accepted an invitation to dinner. Christian women who live this compromising life-style cannot be called "godly," because they are living in contradiction to God's standards. The same is true, of course, of single men.

Unfortunately, some women have been convinced that they should aggressively pursue men. One young man told me about meeting a single woman in church one Sunday. She was new to the city and had not yet met any friends. Her father was a pastor in another state, and she seemed like a nice person. After visiting with her at church, he invited her to go out to dinner the following Friday night.

It would have been a lovely evening except that after dinner, she thought it her duty to provide coffee and "dessert": an intimate sexual invitation to her apartment. This young man was surprised and shocked that his good intentions were leading him down the path toward sexual immorality. He closed the evening abruptly and left his date safely at her front door.

THE IMPORTANCE OF SEXUAL PURITY

The Bible has much to say about the importance of sexual purity in singleness. In Paul's day, Corinth was known for prostitution and sexual perversion—sort of a first-century San Francisco. The sexually permissive Corinthian culture was a source of great temptation and struggle to the Christian believers in that city. To them, Paul wrote:

> Flee from sexual immorality. All other sins a man commits are outside his body, but he who sins sexually sins against his own body. Do you not know that your body is a temple of the Holy Spirit, who is in you, whom you have received from God? You are not your own; you were bought at a price. Therefore honor God with your body. (1 Corinthians 6:18-20)

We are not supposed to expose ourselves to immorality but are commanded to flee from it. This is because when we commit sexual immorality we are sinning against our body, which does not belong to us, but to Christ, who paid for us with his own blood.

With passion and earnestness equaling Paul's, Peter urges Christians to lead upright, blameless lives:

> Dear friends, I urge you, as aliens and strangers in the world, to abstain from sinful desires, which war against your soul. Live such good lives among the pagans that, though they accuse you of doing wrong, they may see your good deeds and glorify God on the day he visits us. (1 Peter 2:11-12)

In his letter to the church in Thessalonica, Paul repeats his message urging the believers to abstain from sexual immorality:

> It is God's will that you should be sanctified: that you should avoid sexual immorality; that each of you should learn to control his own body in a way that is holy and honorable, not in passionate lust like the heathen, who do not know God. (1 Thessalonians 4:3-5)

How does a woman "control her own body" in a holy and honorable way? Where do you draw the line in sexual intimacy? As Dr. James Dobson so aptly described in a broadcast on singles and sexuality, sex is progressive in nature, like a river. It may start as a gentle, slow-flowing stream, but it gains tremendous momentum as it follows its course until it is a rapidly running river, perhaps even a torrent. Similarly, physical contact may start out mild, but it quickly leads downstream to intercourse.

Whether we eat or drink or whatever we do, our lives are to bring glory to God (1 Corinthians 10:31). If you find yourself in a troublesome situation where your purity is endangered, ask yourself, *Is there a way to handle this that will bring glory to God?* If there is not, back out fast.

What did Paul say to do when facing sexual temptation? Flee! Escape, run, desert! One of the participants on the radio broadcast put it this way: "If you never start something, you never have to end it." In other words, if you avoid the little moves, you'll avoid heavier temptations.

Paul flatly advises that "it is good for a man not to touch a woman" (1 Corinthians 7:1-2, NKJV). According to Paul, a legitimate and often compelling reason for a couple to marry is to be able to engage in sexual relations morally, within marriage. This passage clearly instructs us that sexual relations outside marriage are immoral.

WHY NOT, IF WE'RE IN LOVE?

We often hear, "Why shouldn't we have sex? We love each other and we're going to get married anyway."

Love and impending marriage are never a proper justification for disobeying God's standard about immorality!

If for no other reason, we should obey God's commandments because he is worthy of our obedience. But there are other reasons not to engage in sex outside marriage.

First, love is patient; love can wait. Ask yourself if it's love or lust you feel for each other. If you feel you simply cannot wait, perhaps your relationship is not based on the kind of love that lasts.

Second, you have no guarantee that you will get married. Any number of things could arise to prevent you from marrying. As Proverbs 27:1 tells us, "Do not boast about tomorrow, for you do not know what a day may bring forth."

Third, by having sex before marriage, you are taking away from the beauty of your wedding night. You are stealing from tomorrow, much like a child who secretly unwraps her Christmas presents before Christmas and then feels let down on Christmas morning.

Finally, if you and your fiancé are immoral, you have already become one physically. If you do not marry, you will need to be torn from each other. If you do marry, you will have set a precedent for immorality in your relationship. Your premarital actions will have dealt a blow to the respect you have for each other.

When Tim and I were doing research for our book *The Act of Marriage,* we conducted a survey with twenty-three hundred couples to gain information about sexual problems and enjoyment among Christian couples. From this survey we learned that most couples who had engaged in premarital sex thought that if they could begin again, they would remain virgins until marriage. They felt that premarital sex had robbed them of the beautiful mystery surrounding the marriage bed.

DON'T SELL YOURSELF SHORT

With accountability and forethought, single women *can* lead lives of moral purity. In the loving scrutiny of godly friends and spiritual authorities to whom they are accountable, single women can find a life preserver in the flood of immorality that is sweeping across our nation.

I hope you will take every precaution to maintain your purity. It is much harder to swim upstream than down, and many simply don't have the strength to do it. Forethought involves acknowledging your weaknesses, establishing a "line" you will not cross, and planning an escape route if you need it.

One young man on the Focus on the Family broadcast said that when he stays in hotels he calls the desk and asks that movies be blocked from his room. As he wisely recognizes, Christians who want to enjoy the peace that accompanies purity must make hard decisions in advance in order to avoid the "path of regret."

Women must recognize their individual worth and

respect themselves enough not to sell themselves short. Never let the longing for intimacy lead you to behavior that will ultimately undermine or even keep you from the closeness you desire. When you strive for purity when tempted, you will gain respect from yourself as well as from others—including your future husband!

We are the products of our thinking. If our thought lives are filled with soap operas, sleazy romance books, popular magazines and movies, and the lyrics of much contemporary music, we are setting ourselves up for moral failure. We may soon long for the exciting romance we read about or watch, even though entertainment romance has nothing to do with reality; and we'll be tempted to focus on what we do not have rather than on what we do have. As Peter said, there is a war being waged against our souls (1 Peter 2:11), and we mustn't let ourselves be taken in by the pressures and powers that would lead us astray. There have already been too many casualties in the sexual war.

We need to replace thoughts of lust, envy, jealousy, and covetousness with the thoughts Paul describes in Philippians 4:8: thoughts that are noble, just, pure, lovely, good, virtuous, and praiseworthy. The thought life is one battlefield that is extremely difficult to command, particularly if we have already let it become undisciplined. Nevertheless, any effort made in the battle for the mind will be rewarded, and God will help you and give you the strength to overcome. We must cultivate the practice of listening to the Lord and not the world.

The question single women must ask themselves is, How serious am I in my desire to lead a pure, blameless, honorable life? For many women this is a tremendous challenge, but each of us has the responsibility to do all we can to avoid temptation and exercise self-control. We are ultimately responsible for the decisions we make.

HEALING THE SCARS

It grieves me to think of the innumerable victims of the sexual war being waged around us. Countless women feel victimized and cheapened by men who have used them and their bodies and subsequently abandoned them. Even when pregnancy or disease do not result, there are emotional scars against which no condom can protect.

The desire for intimacy felt by many single women cannot be satisfied by illicit sex, which only leads to feelings of low self-respect, depression, and despair. A woman who has been "pawed over" by men will feel like used merchandise. Far from being fulfilled, she will know the hurt of short-lived, deceptive intimacy. As if that were not enough, studies indicate that couples who have been sexually active before marriage are likely to have marital problems resulting from their immorality.

You can only give away your virginity once. If you are still a virgin, guard your virginity. If you have already lost it, you need to know that you are forgiven in Christ. Psalm 103:12 reassures us that "as far as the east is from the west, so far has he removed our transgressions from us." Stay close to the Lord and become familiar with his grace and forgiveness, which has no limitations. You do not have to relive your past wrongs. You may no longer be a virgin, but you can establish moral purity and chastity *today* and remain pure with God's help.

Think of Paul, who, as a former persecutor of the church, was responsible for the death of numerous Christians. Can you imagine the guilt he must have faced when he came to Christ and recognized the sin of his earlier actions? But Paul repented, sought to make amends to those who had suffered at his hands, and went on. Much of his success was a result of his ability to live each day unencumbered by the events of his past.

In my favorite scene from the film *Chariots of Fire,* Eric

Liddell sets off in a race, stumbles, and stands up again with renewed strength and purpose, coming from behind to win. That demonstration of his character is a wonderful example for all of us. It is God's desire that we be winners in the race of life. Forgetting the sins of our past, we must move forward with renewed zeal and determination.

IF ONLY I WERE MARRIED

We all give in to the temptation to envy and compare ourselves with others whose lives seem perfect. I know married women who long for the peacefulness and flexibility of single women. I know single women who long for the security and commitment of marriage. The truth is that there are advantages and difficulties in either status. Marriage is no elixir to heal the "ills" of singleness, nor is singleness a guarantee of a carefree, independent, exciting life, as some assert.

While it is true that God designed marriage to help solve the human problem of loneliness, we should see that marriage is only a season in a woman's life. Those who marry on earth will not remain married to each other in heaven. "At the resurrection," Jesus told his disciples, "people will neither marry nor be given in marriage; they will be like the angels in heaven" (Matthew 22:30). (Whether this statement brings you relief or disappointment depends on your present situation!)

The only marriage that will exist in heaven is the marriage of Christ and his bride, the church. God is not going to abolish marriage completely, because you and I, as members of the church universal, will be joined eternally to our bridegroom, Jesus Christ. No earthly spouse could compare with him. You and I will want him and him only in heaven. And, joy of joys, he will be eternally ours, as we will be eternally his!

Until the time God brings you to your future husband—

if marriage is in his plan for you—there are many lessons you can learn and wonderful experiences that you can enjoy at this time in your life. You never know what tomorrow may bring, and you may not be single for much longer. It would be wise to prepare for future possibilities. In Proverbs 6:6-8 we read: "Go to the ant, you sluggard; consider its ways and be wise! It has no commander, no overseer or ruler, yet it stores its provisions in summer and gathers its food at harvest."

"I want to learn how to cook, clean, and balance a budget before I get married," one young lady commented. Others have vital character areas they want to master before marriage. But simply working on growing in love and all of its attributes—patience, kindness, selflessness, forbearance, trust, hope, endurance—would keep us all busy for a lifetime. There's always room for growth.

Roommates are often beneficial in helping single women overcome loneliness. Having a roommate can teach you flexibility, consideration for others, and teamwork as you manage a house together. There are plenty of life skills single women can and should develop while they have the opportunity. Furthering your education, gaining professional experience, making wise financial investments, purchasing a car or house—these are but a few challenges you should not necessarily put on hold for some future day when you may be married. Whether you marry or remain single, these experiences are invaluable, and the lessons you learn will serve you throughout your lifetime.

A multitude of activities and ministries are especially well suited to single women. Weekend excursions with friends, a trip to Europe, missions in a foreign country, a job that requires travel, or helping needy families with baby-sitting are but a few of the activities readily available to single women but always difficult for married women with children. God calls each of us in different directions at different stages in our lives. Your time of singleness should be an exciting season as you discover what role God has for you.

THE SECRET TO FULFILLMENT

Let's look at one concept that is central to the single woman's fulfillment and happiness. It's not a secret formula, a quick solution, or a three-step strategy to attaining peace and satisfaction. It's a simple idea, and an old one, for Paul discussed it two thousand years ago in the book of Philippians. The concept can be expressed in one word: *contentment.* Paul wrote:

> I have learned to be content whatever the circumstances. I know what it is to be in need, and I know what it is to have plenty. I have learned the secret of being content in any and every situation, whether well fed or hungry, whether living in plenty or in want. I can do everything through him who gives me strength. (Philippians 4:11-13)

Contentment, or satisfaction, is a rare commodity these days. Contentment doesn't come with the wave of a magic wand, for Paul had to learn how to be content. He had to be trained in the grueling school of difficulty in order to gain contentment.

Learning is often a time-consuming, difficult process. Certainly the more complex the information or concept, the more difficult the learning will be. Learning to be content is a lesson many of us take great pains to avoid because it goes against all our natural instincts. Inevitably, however, we must come face to face with our lot in life and decide whether we will be contented or discontented with it. Happiness, however, lies in contentment!

One married woman recently told me about her battle for contentment:

When I was single, I used to think that if only I were married I would be happy. Then I got married and I began to think that if I just had children I would be happy. Once I had children I thought to myself that if only we lived in a house, not an apartment, I would be happy. But then we moved into a house, and soon I began to think that if only we had a bigger, nicer house I would be happy. I've come to the realization that I must be content with what I have, because wherever I am in life, there will always be something or someone I think will satisfy me but which really won't.

Endowed as we are with expansive imaginations, you and I could always dream up a more amplified, richer state or possession for which to long—something we suppose would really make us fulfilled. But such longings breed an inability to be satisfied, and dissatisfaction ruins the quality of our lives.

Contentment, on the other hand, enhances our enjoyment of life on earth and allows us to enjoy the richness and blessings around us now. Paul writes in 1 Timothy 6:6-8: "Godliness with contentment is great gain. For we brought nothing into the world, and we can take nothing out of it. But if we have food and clothing, we will be content with that."

We may have all that we need to be happy, but if we are consumed with the "bigger is better" mind-set, we will never be satisfied. It is said that "discontentment makes rich men poor, while contentment makes poor men rich." Which will you choose?

Paul wrote that he learned to be content in all circumstances. We, too, can be content in good times and bad, because Christ strengthens us and fortifies our inner person. As we are filled with this faith and hope, we will have little trouble enduring what Paul referred to as "light and momentary troubles" (2 Corinthians 4:17). For me, the easiest way to be content in trying circumstances is to trust God, to believe that he really is who he says he is—our provider and the almighty one for whom nothing is too difficult (Jeremiah 32:17).

There are times when our world looks pretty bleak. In those times I think of Paul's words, "We live by faith, not by sight" (2 Corinthians 5:7). If we trust God with the salvation of our souls and eternal life, shouldn't we trust him for the present, which endures for only a little time? We must learn to trust God with every aspect of our daily lives.

If you learn contentment as a single woman, you will have gained a tremendous quality that will support you throughout your life.

PROMISES FOR PROVISION

Contentment, however, does not mean having a fatalistic approach to life that says, "Whatever's going to happen is going to happen. There's nothing I can do about it, so I might as well accept it!" That certainly was not Paul's approach, nor should it be yours. Faith in God's promises is far different from fatalistic pessimism.

The promises of God can be compared to checks that have been written to us but which we must take to the bank to endorse and cash. Discovering and claiming God's promises makes for a life of excitement and great fulfillment! I cannot think of a life more thrilling than the life of faith in our loving Creator. We can trust him completely.

The Bible is full of God's promises to provide for his children. I would encourage single women to meditate on and claim those promises. Our faith assures us that God is good and that his plans for our lives are equally good. I hope that whether you are single or married, you will be inspired to trust God with your future.

There are too many promises in Scripture for me to list

them all, but here are a selected few for your meditation. In Philippians 4:19, God promises to meet our needs—physical, emotional, and spiritual. The prophet Isaiah wrote that the Lord longs to be gracious to us (Isaiah 30:18). In Matthew 6:25-34 Jesus tells his disciples not to worry by reminding them that the heavenly Father feeds even the birds of the air, and that we are of much greater worth than sparrows!

God values us and longs for us to be happy, to have what we truly need. As Paul reasons, "He who did not spare his own Son, but gave him up for us all—how will he not also, along with him, graciously give us all things?" (Romans 8:32).

I believe single women can cherish the thought of marriage and be content at the same time. Through Christ we can do all things. We can trust that the God who made us knows our hearts and intends to fulfill our desires *in his time.* "Delight yourself in the LORD and he will give you the desires of your heart. . . . Be still before the LORD and wait patiently for him" (Psalm 37:4, 7). As Solomon wisely noted, "There is a time for everything, and a season for every activity under heaven" (Ecclesiastes 3:1).

COMPLETE IN CHRIST

It is easy to feel that life is on hold if we're single. It's as if we stand poised, waiting for marriage before punching in our time card, not realizing that the time clock is already running. Life has begun, and as individuals we are complete even if as singles we may not feel that way.

Single women must not let themselves be overcome by the "if only I had" or "if only I were" syndrome. God's Word tells us that in Christ, *we are complete.* "For in Christ all the fullness of the Deity lives in bodily form, and you have been given fullness in Christ, who is the head over every power and authority" (Colossians 2:9-10).

Before we knew Christ, we were not complete. We had a God-shaped vacuum within our souls. Constantly on the lookout for satisfaction and the "missing link" to real life, we found ourselves still searching for meaning after short-lived pleasures. We did not find lasting meaning, satisfaction, and completion until we came to Christ.

When a woman meets Christ, she has met her Savior and the lover of her soul. He completes her with an eternal love. God says, "I have loved you with an everlasting love; I have drawn you with loving-kindness" (Jeremiah 31:3). As believers in Christ, we must continually renew our love for our Lord, who loved us so much that he died in our place in order to bring us to him!

Colossians 2:3 tells us that all the treasures of wisdom and knowledge are hidden in Christ. Why has God hidden the treasures in Christ? God is so unlike us. Most of us flaunt our assets and good qualities for all to see. Why doesn't God do the same?

Perhaps the answer lies in the fact that God does not throw his pearls before swine. He will not give us a treasure that we will neglect or ruin. And because God is pleased by our faith in him, he wants to see just how much we trust his goodness and believe his promises.

When we show God that we earnestly desire him and his gifts, he fills us with treasures of unspeakable worth and incomparable value. These treasures come in many forms; one very big one is the perfection of our character. And when we delight ourselves in the Lord, he will give us the desires of our hearts.

It is natural for women to desire marriage, because God created women with such a desire. But for single women I have some encouraging words from a book written over twenty years ago:

> Do not be afraid to give God everything—even your deepest longings and desires. He will set you at liberty from the frustrations of human desire. He will beautify

your character and personality. He will make you a very much more wonderful person than you are. And you will be much better prepared for a happy marriage should he eventually bring that your way.[3]

SINGLE LOVE AND SERVICE

Eugenia Price writes of Miriam, Moses' sister, whose story is told throughout the first books of the Old Testament. Miriam, a single woman, served God among the Israelites so faithfully that her funeral was celebrated in the most solemn and reverent manner for thirty days:

> Perhaps no one asked Miriam's hand in marriage, perhaps she was not attractive; surely, the Bible gives no inference that she was ever married. But she gathered all the incompleteness of her years—her loneliness, her childlessness, her resentment, into a redemptive song of praise and service to the God she loved and who can speak now to every lonely woman who will ever bemoan her lot. Miriam has earned her right to remind us that an unmarried woman *can* live creatively and fully because, as she sang that day on the freedom side of the Red Sea, "He hath triumphed gloriously."[4]

Miriam served God, but she found fulfillment in loving God. In God's eyes, no amount of "Christian service" can ever replace the simple and pure love we can offer him as his children. God's preeminent commandments are to love him wholly and to love our neighbors as ourselves (Matthew 22:37-39). No amount of work for Christ can replace love. Instead of substituting for love, our work should be a result of our loving and thankful hearts. We see this clearly in Jesus' words to the church in Ephesus:

> I know your deeds, your hard work and your persever-

> ance. I know that you cannot tolerate wicked men, that you have tested those who claim to be apostles but are not, and have found them false. You have persevered and have endured hardships for my name, and have not grown weary. Yet I hold this against you: *You have forsaken your first love.* Remember the height from which you have fallen! Repent and do the things you did at first. If you do not repent, I will come to you and remove your lampstand from its place. (Revelation 2:2-5, italics mine)

Loving God is serious business. The church at Ephesus had worked long and hard. They had done mighty works in Jesus' name. But they had fallen out of love with the Savior.

The Christian single woman is called to love God with her whole heart, just as every believer in Christ is. But the single woman has perhaps even greater incentive to find in Christ the riches for which her heart longs. Single women are uniquely endowed with the opportunity to seek and serve Christ without distractions. And although the mere fact that a woman is single does not guarantee that she will seek God earnestly, if she chooses to make herself wholly available to him, she can be used uniquely in God's eternal work. Gien Karssen wrote about this in her book *Getting the Most Out of Being Single: The Gift of Single Womanhood:*

> Some tasks are open *only* to the single woman. A story is told of two female missionaries of the Wycliffe Bible Translators in South America. An Indian chief in Peru told a missionary official, "If you had sent men, we would have killed them on sight. Or if a couple, I'd have killed the man and taken the woman for myself. But what could a great chief do with two harmless girls who insisted on calling him 'brother'?"[5]

It is beautiful to observe examples of women who have yielded their lives to the Master. Such women are undoubtedly highly esteemed by the Lord, whose opinion matters most of all.

Whatever our status in life—whether we're single, engaged, married, divorced, or widowed—we are called to love and serve our God with all of our hearts. The secret to fulfillment and happiness is not marriage, but a life yielded to God in faith. As we trust his love for us, his power to work in and for us, and his great wisdom, we will be at peace.

All women, married or single, must come to the place where there is rest and contentment. We must search out the treasure Christ has for us, finding our completion in Christ.

QUESTIONS
FOR REFLECTION AND DISCUSSION

1. What are some constructive ways in which single women can channel their desire for intimacy?
2. Where should singles draw the line in the area of sexual intimacy?
3. How can women avoid becoming casualties in the sexual war?
4. What are some practical ways in which single women can avoid what has been called "the path of regret"?
5. Why is it important for women to learn contentment?
6. How can single women capitalize on their marital status?

6

We Want to Love and Respect Our Husbands

If you're like me, as a young girl you dreamed of your wedding day for years before it finally arrived. I dreamed about my beautiful white wedding gown and the vast array of flowers spread across the altar. It's funny, but I was so caught up in the lace and beauty I really didn't think much about what kind of man would be waiting at the altar!

But marriage is a partnership, and as we consider marriage, we have to consider the man we have married or may marry. I realize that you may be married, separated, divorced, widowed, or single, and your needs and interests will vary according to your experiences and current situation. It is my hope that this material will meet you at your place of need. God's Word will shed light on all our ways and give us wisdom beyond our years if we will apply our minds and hearts to it (Psalm 119: 99, 105). Let's allow the Word of God to direct our desires for our husbands.

MARRIAGE WAS MEANT TO LAST

Marriage was God's idea, and he has all the directions we need to make marriage work. "Haven't you read," Jesus once asked his disciples, "that at the beginning the Creator 'made them male and female,' and said, 'For this reason a man will leave his father and mother and be united to his wife, and the two will become one flesh'? So they are no longer two, but one. Therefore what God has joined together, let man not separate" (Matthew 19:4-6).

When a man and woman make a marital commitment, they say good-bye to their old lives and hello to new lives of interdependence and sacrifice. Some might wonder why people enter into such a sacrificial relationship, but God created us with an instinctive knowledge of the joy that flows from a sacrifice born of love. "That is what love is," writes John Piper, "the pursuit of our own joy in the joy of the beloved."[1]

In bringing joy to another, we ourselves find joy. This is in direct contrast to a worldly, self-centered "tit-for-tat," "you scratch my back and I'll scratch yours" approach to marriage. As Piper further explains, "Selfishness seeks its own private happiness at the expense of others. Love seeks its happiness in the happiness of the beloved."[2]

Many of us enter marriage with grandiose expectations— we expect that our husbands will bring us flowers, whisper sweet endearments every morning, and never, never direct a harsh word in our direction. These expectations are unrealistic, and many brides have experienced a harsh awakening in the first year of marriage when the honeymoon settles down to reality.

Our expectations in marriage should be, not self-centered, but other-centered. We should not ask what we're going to get out of marriage, but rather what we're going to give.

SIN DESTROYS MARRIAGES
Though God designed a perfect blueprint for marriage, sin marred the materials with which God was

working. As Larry Crabb observed in his book *The Marriage Builder:*

> Sin has made an utter wreck of things. God's original design was that a man and woman should live in fellowship with Him and in a selfless relationship of mutual giving to each other. In such a relationship my love would so thrill my wife that I would feel deeply significant as I realized the joy that my love creates in her; I would exult in the security that her love provides me. She too would find her significance in touching my deepest needs and would enjoy the security of my love for her.[3]

Few people today find such joy and happiness in marriage. Statistics show us that five out of ten marriages end in divorce.

Traditionally, husbands and wives have committed themselves to each other in marriage for better or for worse. Today, however, it seems that there is a new, unspoken approach to marriage: Some enter into the covenant seeing their union not as a marriage of commitment but as one of compatibility or convenience. This attitude has no doubt been encouraged by the widespread no-fault divorce laws, which make divorce legal when either the husband or the wife claims that "irreconcilable differences" have broken down their marriage.

Washington Post reporter Barbara Vobejda remarked: "Baby boom women who are now age 30 to 44 are more likely to be divorced at some time in their lives than any group in American history, part of a pattern of 'remarkable' changes in marriage and divorce that have altered American society dramatically over the last two decades."[4] Authors Arthur J. Norton and Louisa F. Miller have also noted, "Couples are marrying later and they are divorcing and remarrying in numbers that would have been beyond comprehension 25 years ago."[5]

In our race to find happiness, we seem only to have succeeded in tearing ourselves apart. When life gets too hard, society teaches us that we should look for the quickest and easiest way out. Commitments are for the short term, and promises are allowed to be broken for the sake of personal satisfaction.

While sitting in the Chicago airport I overheard two people talking about a wedding they were going to attend. One expressed doubt that this boy and girl would make a good marriage. The other simply shrugged his shoulders and remarked that the bride and groom did not expect it to be a lifetime relationship, but just the start of their adult life. This marriage is defeated before it begins.

How often do people enter marriage these days with the purpose of living to promote the other's good, committing themselves to their spouse for better or for worse, in sickness and in health, till death do them part? Even those couples who survive without getting divorced are not guaranteed carefree, "low-maintenance" marriages. Without exception, marriage requires vigilance, diligence, and painstaking effort on the part of both partners. Whether it comes in the form of alcohol, pornography, violence, lust, or something else, sin will destroy a home and marriage.

MARRIAGE BEGINS WITH RELATIONSHIP

Before we can love and respect our husbands, we must form a relationship. Beginning in the book of Genesis, we see that marriage was instituted by God to meet a man's need of a companion. God had given Adam animals as companions and subjects to rule over, "but for Adam no suitable helper was found" (Genesis 2:20). Adam was not complete, and God said he needed a helper.

That's when Eve entered the scene. Eve was very well

suited to Adam, and she brought him great delight. The Creator could have created another man for fellowship or given him an animal for a partner, but neither would have been a helper suitable for him. Man needed a helper who would be able to give him completion and to replenish the earth. This was to be a special creation. Man was formed of the dust of the ground, but woman was fashioned from the rib of the man. Eve came into existence from something already created; in other words, she was an extension, or part of, man.

I find it interesting to note that God "created" man, but "fashioned" woman. The word *fashioned* comes from the Hebrew word meaning "to build" or "to design." God had a special blueprint and design for woman, so he fashioned her into what he wanted her to be. Could it be that God took extra care in making woman, so she could be a fairer sex and a feminine beauty? She was designed to complement the man, not replace him.

Although the honeymoon in the Garden of Eden was idyllic, delightful, and satisfying, sin slithered in through the serpent, destroying paradise for the first couple and all their descendants. Since that day, every man and woman has suffered the ramifications of the first moral failure. You and I are flawed. We will not be the angels our husbands thought us to be. Our husbands will not be the charming princes we hoped they were. Marriage begins with an attraction for the opposite sex that turns to love, but that is not enough. Marriage must be undergirded with a commitment to make this relationship last. That is why marriage must be entered into cautiously and prayerfully and vigilantly guarded ever after.

In order to love and respect our husbands, we must first understand our role as women. God designed woman to correspond to the man in all areas: physically, emotionally, mentally, and spiritually. Scripture tells us that "man did not come from woman, but woman from man; neither was man created for woman, but woman for man" (1 Corinthians 11:8-9). Unless we accept the Bible's teaching that woman was created for man, we cannot begin to follow God's plan for happy marriages. Denial of this foundational truth may be the first step of rebellion against God's plan for happiness in marriage.

FEMINISM'S TOXIC INFLUENCE

Our world is reeling from the ravages of feminist rebellion against God and God-given authorities. Women are taught to resent male authority as well as every other authority in their lives. The liberal feminist line teaches that women and men are interchangeable, and some in our churches are misinterpreting Galatians 3:28 ("There is neither Jew nor Greek, slave nor free, male nor female, for you are all one in Christ Jesus") to mean that there is no difference between men and women with regard to spiritual authority. However, a contextual look at this passage reveals that it speaks of equal access to God and equal entitlement to God's spiritual promises and blessings. It does not live up to the feminist ideal of identity of function.

A man's role as leader is threatened when the woman refuses to give him the support he needs in the challenging task of undertaking godly leadership. We continue to see women usurp men's roles in the home and in the church, which squelches men's ability to lead, protect, care for, and provide for their families, churches, and communities.

But sometimes men are their own enemy in the struggle over roles. They are often as confused as women as to what their roles should be. Afraid of being regarded as politically incorrect and chauvinistic, men often retreat into the safety zone of indifference, listlessness, and apathy. I believe that men must rise above the worldly criticism and solve this problem by developing and living according to biblical convictions on their calling and responsibility as men, regardless of whether or not they get the encouragement from women to do so.

I recently heard an interesting story that aptly illustrates the influence of the women's movement on roadside manners. A male friend was driving down a congested freeway in northern California a few years ago, and he spotted a car on the shoulder of the road. As he approached the car, he noticed that there were two attractive women standing beside the disabled vehicle. The man was surprised that no one had stopped to help these women until he got close enough to read the bumper sticker on their car. It read: Support Women's Liberation!

It appears that those women got what they asked for. When women ask to be liberated from men, they are forfeiting help on the occasions when they really need it.

Men and women are not interchangeable. We need each other as men and as women, not as androgynous human beings. Most women are not looking for emasculated, wimpy men. What do women want in a husband? Let's look at several important characteristics.

WE WANT GODLY HUSBANDS

We want to love and respect our husbands because they are godly, but the biblical model of a godly man in leadership and a wife who submits is not often followed in today's world. "The Western world," writes James Dobson, "stands at a great crossroads in its history. It is my opinion that our very survival as a people will depend upon the presence or absence of masculine leadership in millions of homes. . . . I believe, with everything within me, that husbands hold the keys to the preservation of the family."[6]

I believe women want a husband who will be loving and respectful to them and at the same time exhibit the strength and courage necessary to lead the family. The

Bible gives us countless examples of the disastrous consequences of violating the principle of male leadership. With Adam and Eve, we see that Adam, as firstborn, should have provided Eve with spiritual leadership, especially since Eve's open and trusting nature made her susceptible to Satan's lure.

Interestingly, statistics show that more women than men read Christian books, teach Sunday school, and ask spiritual questions. When not under God-given spiritual authority, this potential strength in women becomes a great weakness. Have you ever noticed that the vast majority of fortune-tellers are women? A recent television commercial advertising a psychic telephone service showed a series of satisfied female customers. Perhaps this is a reflection of women's openness to the spiritual world.

When the serpent approached Eve, it was not because she was less spiritual than Adam, but because she was more emotionally responsive to misdirection. A modern woman's susceptibility to misdirection is the same as Eve's, no matter how logical or brilliant she may be. It is partially *because* of the women's interest in knowledge that God directs the husband to be the spiritual head of the family. Remember, a woman's weaknesses are pride and an insatiable desire for knowledge, both of which make her easily deceived. The husband's responsibility for spiritual leadership is a grace gift given by God for the wife's protection from deception.[7]

WE WANT COMMUNICATIVE HUSBANDS

One of a woman's greatest needs and desires is to have healthy, open communication with her husband. As we have already learned, the goals and styles of communication differ greatly between men and women. More than one bride has been disappointed by the change she notices in her husband's communication following marriage. In her husband's eyes, they have already communicated. *She knows I love her,* he may reason, *so why do I have to tell her again and again?*

Communication problems between husbands and wives are not limited to the romantic aspect of life. Because women are typically endowed with the ability and desire to communicate abundantly in order to foster intimacy, it is not uncommon for women to be frustrated with the low level and/or quality of communication between them and their husbands.

What causes poor communication in couples? My husband, Tim, and I discussed this topic in our book *Spirit-Controlled Family Living.* We noted that differing perspectives and primary interests as well as differing temperaments are among the causes of communication troubles between husbands and wives.

For instance, if the husband is at work eight to ten hours of his day and comes home to his wife whose primary focus is the home, they may find they have to work at finding something in common to talk about. She wants to talk about the broken dishwasher, and he wants to mull over his slim chances for promotion. Because of this lack of commonality, it is very important that a couple develops shared interests. Regularly praying and studying the Word of God together as well as developing friendships with Christians are some of the Christ-related activities that enhance communication between spouses. Couples should learn to do something together.

Other keys to effective communication are:

- Learn to understand your partner and the differences between you.
- Accept your partner unconditionally and cheerfully.
- Plan a suitable time to talk to your partner.
- Introduce negative subjects tactfully.
- Speak the truth in love and with grace.

- Allow for reaction time; don't press for instant decisions or feedback.
- Never argue or defend yourself by attacking and saying "You always . . . !" or "You never . . . !"
- Pray about your discussion and decisions.

If you're facing a problem in your marriage, talk about it with your husband. Once you have communicated a matter to your husband, you have, through prayer, a higher court of appeal to which you can turn. Prayer and submission to your husband bring you two benefits: First, you receive the blessing of God on your problem, and second, you can "back off" because you have stated the issue. By prayer you can, in faith, anticipate a change, but it must be instituted by God, not you.[8]

If you and your spouse have had difficulties with communication, don't lose heart. I have seen marriages with terrible communication problems turn around once both spouses understood and committed themselves to open, loving, uplifting communication. Remember, good communication may need to begin with you.

When you find yourself in a potentially explosive situation, realize that it is good to express your feelings and frustrations honestly, as long as you do it without accusing or attacking. Your goal in communication should be to pursue understanding, love, forgiveness, peace, and healing. Always be ready to offer an apology, if necessary, and forgiveness.

As one pastor put it, we are to teach our mouths and hearts until we can say the right thing at the right time in the right way for the right purpose. Simple, but not easy. Keep Ephesians 4:29 in mind: "Do not let any unwholesome talk come out of your mouths, but only what is helpful for building others up according to their needs, that it may benefit those who listen."

WE WANT FAITHFUL HUSBANDS

We women do not want our husbands to lust after other women. We want husbands who will be faithful to their own wives; we want our husbands to know how to discipline themselves and control their passions. Once a man has proven his ability to lead himself by the principles of God's Word, then he will be able to lead his children and household as well.

Our society steadily encourages men to indulge their whims and "live it up," so for men to conquer the urges that would dominate them, they must be strong in God's Word and in his strength. When a man has disciplined himself for the purpose of godliness (1 Timothy 4:7), he will be able to lead his family, society, and the church as well.

A single woman approaching marriage would be wise to consider how her intended husband is able to discipline his own passions. Is he capable of being faithful and committed before marriage? If so, he has the capability to be faithful to his future wife.

WE WANT CARING HUSBANDS

Women desire security, protection, and peace, and we often search for these qualities in our husbands. Recent polls have shown that more and more, women are looking to government as their provider. Our present welfare system encourages single women not to marry. Because men have failed in their responsibility to provide for their wives, there is a growing attitude among women from broken marriages that they can depend on government more than on men. Women favor bigger government because they see that they can no longer count on men to provide their needs with regard to money, home, and child care.

While it is a man's mandate to provide for and protect his wife, we must realize that ultimately our security, protection, and peace come from the Lord. In *The Marriage*

Builder, Larry Crabb writes about men and women providing each other with security and significance while affirming that "personal needs for security and significance can be genuinely and fully met only in relationship with the Lord Jesus Christ."[9] Only God can be our unfailing source of security, and he is: "And He shall be the stability of your times, a wealth of salvation, wisdom, and knowledge; the fear of the LORD is his treasure (Isaiah 33:6, NASB)."

If you have been rejected or abandoned by the husband of your youth, if you are longing for the appearance of a man in your life, or if you are happily married, I have an encouraging Scripture from the LORD. It applies to us wherever we are in life:

> "For your Maker is your husband—the LORD Almighty is his name—the Holy One of Israel is your Redeemer; he is called the God of all the earth. The LORD will call you back as if you were a wife deserted and distressed in spirit—a wife who married young, only to be rejected," says your God. "For a brief moment I abandoned you, but with deep compassion I will bring you back. In a surge of anger I hid my face from you for a moment, but with everlasting kindness I will have compassion on you," says the LORD your Redeemer. (Isaiah 54:5-8)

We must always remember, whatever our circumstances, that God desires the firstfruits of our hearts. He wants our love and trust. We need to look to him to meet all of our needs.

We desire a husband who cares for us as Christ does. Our interactions with him will be characterized by compassion and understanding, kindness, gentleness, thoughtfulness, grace, and humility. In order to thrive, a woman needs a husband who is truly Christlike. In all his strength and manliness, our Lord Jesus was never insensitive or callous. He had compassion on the distressed and calls to us this way: "Come to me, all you who are weary and burdened, and I will give you rest. Take my yoke upon you and learn from me, for I am gentle and humble in heart, and you will find rest for your souls. For my yoke is easy and my burden is light" (Matthew 11:28-30).

God cares for us with tenderness. He promises his people that he will give us shepherds according to his heart, who will feed us with knowledge and understanding (Jeremiah 3:15). Many a woman longs for a man who can shepherd her life and feed her with knowledge and understanding. As Christ loved the church, husbands are to love their wives and actively pursue their wives' spiritual maturity and purity of character in the sight of the Lord.

WE WANT CONFIDANTS AND PARTNERS

A woman also wants a best friend and life partner in her husband. Nothing is more frustrating to a woman than feeling that she is merely what George Gilder, author of *Men and Marriage,* refers to as the "matrix," or source, of her husband's pleasure. Nor is a wife content to be regarded simply as the caretaker of her husband's children and house. A woman does not fare well when treated as a means to an end or when given the dregs of a man's time.

As women, we want to be enjoyed for our whole person. And God, our eternal defender, speaks on our behalf to men:

> The LORD is acting as the witness between you and the wife of your youth, because you have broken faith with her, though she is your partner, the wife of your marriage covenant. Has not the LORD made them one? In flesh and spirit they are his. And why one? Because he was seeking godly offspring. So guard yourself in your

spirit, and do not break faith with the wife of your youth. (Malachi 2:14-15)

As Christian women, we also want to have a spiritual "partnership" with our husbands in our service for the Lord. King Solomon, the wisest man ever to live, believed in partnership:

Two are better than one, because they have a good return for their work: If one falls down, his friend can help him up. But pity the man who falls and has no one to help him up! Also, if two lie down together, they will keep warm. But how can one keep warm alone? Though one may be overpowered, two can defend themselves. A cord of three strands is not quickly broken. (Ecclesiastes 4:9-12)

Priscilla and Aquila were an outstanding New Testament example of a husband and wife team. Not only did they share their profession, tentmaking, but they were also spiritual partners in the gospel. In fact, among his closing comments in his letter to the Romans, Paul wrote, "Greet Priscilla and Aquila, my fellow workers in Christ Jesus. They risked their lives for me. Not only I but all the churches of the Gentiles are grateful to them" (Romans 16:3-4). Indeed, these two conducted themselves in a manner worthy of the gospel, "in one spirit, contending as one . . . for the faith of the gospel" (Philippians 1:27).

WE WANT SEXUAL LOVE

When my husband and I wrote *The Act of Marriage*, we wanted to establish the scriptural basis for sexual love. Sadly, the entertainment world has influenced us to the point that many people subconsciously associate sex with perversion. But the act of marriage is that beautiful and intimate relationship shared uniquely by a husband and wife in the privacy of their love—and it is sacred. In a real sense, God designed men and women for that relationship. Proof that it is a sacred experience appears in God's first commandment to man: "Be fruitful, and multiply, and replenish the earth" (Genesis 1:28, KJV). That charge was given before sin entered the world; therefore, lovemaking and procreation were ordained and enjoyed while man continued in his original state of innocence.[10]

Sex is only perverse when it is immoral, and it is immoral when it is outside the bond of marriage. Within marriage, however, it is a beautifully uniting experience that God created for men and women to fully enjoy. King Solomon, who in the Proverbs frequently warned his son against the dangers of immoral sexual relations, encouraged his son in the following way: "May your fountain be blessed, and may you rejoice in the wife of your youth. A loving doe, a graceful deer—may her breasts satisfy you always, may you ever be captivated by her love" (Proverbs 5:18-19).

The Bible says, "Marriage should be honored by all, and the marriage bed kept pure, for God will judge the adulterer and all the sexually immoral" (Hebrews 13:4). God created sexual love to be a beautiful expression of union between a husband and wife. Tragically, it has been distorted and twisted. Promiscuity before marriage and infidelity after marriage devastates men, women, the family unit, and ultimately, our nation. Unfortunately, the church is not immune to promiscuity. This must grieve the Lord greatly.

Why is it that such a unique and beautiful gift has become a cause of such grief and pain? In their book *When Two Walk Together,* Richard and Mary Strauss note the regrettable frequency of sexual difficulties within marriage:

> Rare are the husband and wife who have not at times bounced unhappily over rocks in the road of marital

lovemaking. It is an enigma that something so enjoy-
able should be the source of so much tension and conflict, yet many testify that it is, and we are among
them.[11]

There are, of course, many reasons for unfulfilling, frustrating experiences in sexual love. Often problems arise
because women don't understand that men differ from
them sexually just as they differ physically, socially, mentally,
and spiritually. Men are speedy microwaves, while women
tend to be slow-cooking Crockpots. Men are aroused by
sight; women are aroused by touch and tenderness. Unless
we understand and expect these differences, we set ourselves up for disappointment, frustration, and confusion.

Lovemaking means different things to men and women.
In *The Act of Marriage,* Tim and I wrote about the meaning
of sexual love to men. Sex satisfies a man's sex drive, fulfills
his manhood, enhances his love for his wife, reduces friction in the home, and provides one of life's most exciting
experiences. A wife's needs, however, are not identical to
her husband's. In addition to fulfilling her womanhood,
sexual love reassures her of her husband's love.

A woman desires five kinds of love from her husband:
companionship love, compassionate love, romantic love,
affectionate love, and passionate love. Women need to be
romanced, and men generally couldn't care less about flowers and moonlight. While men relate most readily to the
need for passionate love, a man who does not provide his
wife with companionship, compassion, romance, and affec-
tion may wonder why she is reluctant to provide him with
the passionate love he desires.

WE WANT MEN OF VISION
Women want to love and respect husbands who are
firm leaders and protectors. We want to marry men of

vision, men who will grapple with God's calling on their lives until they discover it, and then will spend their lives fulfilling it. We believe the Lord's promise to us in Jeremiah 29:11: "'For I know the plans I have for you,' declares the LORD, 'plans to prosper you and not to harm you, plans to give you hope and a future.'"

We desire to follow men after God's own heart, men who have sought the Lord, found him, and are still pursuing him. Such men live by the truth of Matthew 6:33: "But seek first his kingdom and his righteousness, and all these things will be given to you as well."

Why is there a decline in male spiritual leadership today? What can Christian women do to help reverse this trend?

First, we must restore the Bible's rightful position in our lives. While it has always been important for God's people to write his Word upon the tablets of our hearts, it is especially crucial that we do so today while our country is declining morally and culturally. God's Word will instruct us in the right way as we go through our days, correct us when we veer off course, and keep us from the many forms of deception that come our way.

You're probably familiar with the saying, "garbage in, garbage out." Every day you and I listen to and watch countless messages of propaganda from the media and entertainment industry. Unless we remain vigilant, we will be swept away with the world's distorted life-styles and philosophies. Every day unsuspecting Christians are led farther and farther away from the truth. The apostle John warned us about this:

> Do not love the world or anything in the world. If anyone loves the world, the love of the Father is not in him. For everything in the world—the cravings of sinful man, the lust of his eyes and the boasting of what he has and does—comes not from the Father but from

the world. The world and its desires pass away, but the man who does the will of God lives forever. (1 John 2:15-17)

WE WANT HUSBANDS WHO LEAD

As Eve was created to complement and complete Adam, Adam was called to be the spiritual head of his family. Regrettably, these concepts find little favor in the eyes of the feminized world. Most feminists would say that marriages should have two heads. Nevertheless, God's plan stands the test of time. In his book *Point Man: How a Man Can Lead a Family,* Steve Farrar discusses the man's role in family leadership:

> Scripture indicates that God holds the man responsible for decisions made in the family, just as the quarterback is responsible for decisions on the field and the airline captain is responsible for decisions in the cockpit.
>
> One clear example is found in Genesis 3:1-13 when Adam and Eve were in the Garden. The account plainly shows that it was Eve who first succumbed to temptation and brought sin into the world. Adam, unfortunately, soon repeated the disobedient act. Yet when God approached them to discuss the matter, *He purposely sought out Adam first.* It would have made more sense for Him to have approached Eve first, unless of course, by the man's headship position, he was ultimately accountable for those choices, just as an executive vice president of marketing is ultimately responsible for the decisions made in his department.[12]

Ultimately it is the man's responsibility to lead his wife and children. If they fail, he is called to account for such failure. With his leadership role comes tremendous responsibility. This is not to imply that the wife is not also to be held accountable for her shortcomings. On the contrary, each of us will one day give an account for our own actions (Romans 14:12). Nevertheless, as the head, the husband has the unique charge of overseeing, guiding, and protecting those whom he is to lead.

Some might argue that many women are as competent as men to lead and make intelligent decisions. Some are even more competent than their husbands. While this observation is true, it misses the point. "The role of the husband," says Elisabeth Elliot, "is the gift of initiation. This is a gift, not earned, not achieved, not dependent on superior intelligence, virtue nor physical prowess, but *assigned* by God."[13]

We must understand that the issue is assignment, not aptitude. F. LaGard Smith also touches on this idea in his recent book, *What Most Women Want: What Few Women Find*. In it he explains that Adam was by birth the firstborn, and therefore the head:

> Birthright—the right of inheritance—came through the firstborn: "That son is the first sign of his father's strength. The right of the firstborn belongs to him" (Deuteronomy 21:17). . . . The headship of the first-born . . . was a matter of arbitrary designation without reference to any subjective factor of qualification for the role.[14]

HOW HUSBANDS ARE TO LEAD

If husbands have been spiritually designed to lead their wives, how are they to do so? The foundation for leadership comes through developing and maintaining a vibrant relationship with the Lord. The quality of a husband's relationship with his wife is directly related to the strength of his relationship with God. When the vertical relationship is healthy, the horizontal relationship will be vibrant also.

Over two hundred years ago, Robert Murray McCheyne wrote to a young ministerial student who was abroad studying German:

> I know you will apply hard to German, but do not forget the culture of the inner man—I mean of the heart. How diligently the cavalry officer keeps his sabre clean and sharp; every stain he rubs off with the greatest care. Remember you are God's sword, His instrument—I trust, a chosen vessel unto Him to bear His name. In great measure, according to the purity and perfection of the instrument, will be the success. It is not great talents God blesses so much as likeness to Jesus. A holy minister is an awful weapon in the hands of God."[15]

As spiritual protectors—not dictators—men are to be vigilant, aggressively seeking the spiritual, emotional, physical welfare of their wives and children, while maintaining a humble and gentle spirit and showing consideration for others.

A woman's relationship with her husband is exquisitely unique and the most intimate of all her relationships. Why shouldn't it be? Marriage is, after all, a picture of Christ and the church. Paul says to wives and husbands:

> As the church submits to Christ, so also wives should submit to their husbands in everything. Husbands, love your wives, just as Christ loved the church and gave himself up for her to make her holy, cleansing her by the washing with water through the word, and to present her to himself as a radiant church, without stain or wrinkle or any other blemish, but holy and blameless. In this same way, husbands ought to love their wives as their own bodies. He who loves his wife loves himself. (Ephesians 5:24-28)

Christian women who know the Scriptures and understand the principle of male leadership can inadvertently turn men away from their God-given role. With sincere intentions we sometimes take it upon ourselves to lead a man to leadership! Prodding and nagging, however, will not persuade or help men return to their God-given place of spiritual leadership. Instead, women's godly lives will convince men to return to their biblical roles on the forefront.

Once men begin to lead, we women must support them. It is tremendously tempting to undermine our husbands' authority when they fail in leadership, but we must turn to God in faith at such times. In wisdom, we can use our influence, our patience, and our nurturing instincts to quietly urge our husbands to positions of leadership as we love and respect them.

HOW WE INFLUENCE OUR HUSBANDS

While the primary focus of this chapter is on husbands, I believe we cannot adequately discuss the subject without coming to a deep realization of the enormous influence a wife has on her husband. We have already seen the influence Eve exercised in her husband's life to their mutual detriment and the harm of all generations to follow. As a wife can influence her husband negatively, she is also able to do so positively. Her position of submission is surprisingly powerful. As women after God's own heart, we are responsible for using our position of influence in our husbands' lives to build, strengthen, encourage, and support them.

In her book *On the Other Side of the Garden,* Virginia Fugate reveals that a wife's influence is felt in four basic areas of her husband's life. The first of these is her husband's masculinity:

Damage a husband's manhood, and he will begin to lose the desire (and confidence) to be a responsible husband. Conversely, protect and support his manhood and he becomes encouraged to be a better leader, provider, and protector.[16]

The second area in which a wife's influence is felt is her husband's initiative to succeed in life:

Her demonstration of trust in his ability to succeed and her appreciation of his efforts strengthen his resolve to be victorious in life's battles. The biblical woman is truly her husband's "better half," as well as his loyal and compassionate friend.

On the other hand, the wife who refuses to fulfill the intended design of helpmate abandons her husband to fight his battles alone. Without a helpmate fit for him, he is vulnerable to a multitude of difficulties. Instead of his helpmate easing the pain of life, her indifference increases his suffering; instead of building his confidence, her lack of support weakens his morale. Rather than assuaging his doubts, her distrustful criticisms increase his insecurity and destroy his initiative. When a wife is a negative influence on her husband, she becomes the "old ball and chain," rather than his "better half."[17]

A third area where Virginia Fugate has noted that a wife plays an influential role is in her husband's major leadership decisions. After establishing the difference between leadership decisions (issues that have a major impact on the entire family) and subordinate decisions (those that follow and successfully implement the policies of the leader), Virginia Fugate makes this observation:

Even though a husband is ultimately responsible for leadership decisions, a wife should remember that she is always in a position to influence those decisions. A wife who knows her husband is assertive and secure in his role as leader may freely express her views and preferences during pre-decision discussions. The wife of a husband who biblically leads his family, can relax in the confidence that her husband will weigh her ideas carefully before making a major decision.[18]

A fourth area in which Virginia Fugate points out that the wife has a lot of influence on her husband concerns spiritual issues. In reference to the instruction in 1 Peter 3 for wives to be submissive to their husbands and to win disobedient husbands through right conduct rather than speech, she notes: "A woman who understands these principles realizes that her influence is spiritually strongest when it is personally weakest."[19] A woman is not called to "fill in" for her spiritually weaker husband. She is to honor and trust God by submitting to him.

> The husband who has a biblical helpmate will often begin to develop his potential for leadership and service in the church. Furthermore, because God protects those who honor Him, the whole nation benefits from biblically functioning homes. All these blessings are possible when a woman trusts God enough to function as a biblical helpmate and to influence her husband only in ways that bring glory and honor to Him.[20]

I would like to close this chapter with Elisabeth Elliot's instructive and inspiring words on biblical leadership and submission:

> Husbands are to love their wives because they are likened to Christ who loved the Church and laid down His life for the Church. He came to redeem her, to

make her pure and holy, to cherish and protect her. The earthly husband's role is a similar one. The wife's role is a complementary one. To adapt herself to his needs, to respond to his initiation, to submit, to receive.

To submit doesn't mean to become a zero. The idea is to acknowledge your head. Every member of a human body obeys the commands given in the head. When the wife acknowledges that her husband is her head, she acknowledges that he is her source, her leader, her authority, and she voluntarily accepts the authority.

She does it gladly, not in rebellion nor resignation, but in obedience to God. Her respect for her husband will not necessarily require that she keep her mouth shut; in fact, if she truly loves and respects him there will be times when she will feel responsible to speak out. But the buck stops with the husband.

The scriptural idea about authority is not bossism, and the scriptural idea of submission is not servility. It's glad and voluntary obedience, each respecting the other, each sacrificing himself for the other.[21]

What is the desire of a woman's heart with regard to her husband? She wants a man she can love and respect whole-heartedly, as the Bible commands her to do.

QUESTIONS
FOR REFLECTION AND DISCUSSION

1. What should women expect to give and receive in marriage?
2. What is God's blueprint for successful marriage?
3. What are some of the ingredients of a good marriage?
4. What characteristics do women desire in their husbands?
5. Why is it important that a wife affirm and support her husband?
6. How can women encourage their husbands in godliness?
7. How can husbands and wives improve their communication?
8. What can we learn about the marital relationship by comparing it to Christ and the church?
9. How is a husband called to exercise spiritual headship over his family?
10. What does it mean for a woman to submit to her husband?

7

We Want to Experience the Beauty of Motherhood

In a recently released movie, a tough-talking police woman goes undercover in a religious community to ferret out a criminal. As she studies the devout people, she asks one young woman about her goals in life. "I want to be married and raise children," the young woman replies.

"Nothing else?" the police woman answers, amazed. "That's all you want to do?"

The young girl smiles sweetly. "Is there anything more important?" she asks.

Most little girls will tell you that when they grow up they want to be mommies. There's nothing more natural. But somewhere during the next fifteen or twenty years that desire becomes muddled. Society and education often turn those natural desires away from that early longing.

Some women have lost sight of the beauty of motherhood and have focused instead on issues of convenience and control. Look carefully at what feminists are promoting, and you will see that only one thing is considered: what the woman wants. If she wants to have sex, she has it, whether or not she is in a position to care for a child. If she does not want to be pregnant, she gets an abortion. If she wants a child, she conceives it, even if it will be fatherless. If she wants to go back to work and leave the child in the care of others, she does so, preferably at public expense. And the schools must promote these female "rights" by aggressively teaching that all kinds of families are equally good.

In this warped view of motherhood, the child's needs are not even mentioned. *Motherhood* used to be a term of honor and responsibility; today it has been reduced to an optional status with an ever-decreasing sphere of influence.

The vast majority of women, thank God, want to raise children with integrity and strong character. We want our children to grow into marriages of their own without having aborted their own children. We want our children to be spared from sexually transmitted diseases and early death from AIDS, drugs, or bullets. Is this too much to ask?

CARING FOR LIFE

Before we look at motherhood itself, we need to look at something in our society that is devaluing the whole concept of giving birth to and nurturing children. I am speaking of abortion.

The beauty of motherhood is impossible unless our children have the fundamental right to life. The joy we take in our children is diminished by the knowledge that in the last twenty years, 28 million babies have legally been put to death in our country.

It is unconscionable that our great nation, founded to protect the individual's right to life, liberty, and the pursuit of happiness, is so quickly recanting its own founding principles! What has happened to the heart of our nation? As you read this, thousands of American women are exercising their "right to choose" as a higher priority over their babies' right to live.

Many women have told me they never fully realized what they were doing when they had abortions. Some may have truly convinced themselves that the child growing within them was a mere piece of tissue; others chose not to investigate but acted impulsively during a crisis. As Randy Alcorn notes in his outstanding book *Pro Life Answers to Pro Choice Arguments,* "Among those scientists who have no vested interests in the abortion issue, there is an overwhelming consensus that human life begins at conception."[1]

But even if there were any doubt about an embryo's humanity, would such a doubt justify the act of abortion? President Ronald Reagan addressed that question: "If we don't know, then shouldn't we morally opt on the side that is life?" the President asked. "If you came upon an immobile body and you yourself could not determine whether it was dead or alive, I think that you would decide to consider it alive until someone could prove it was dead. You wouldn't get a shovel and start covering it up. And I think we should do the same thing with regard to abortion."[2]

Tragically, some women have seared their consciences to the point that they don't care what they are doing. Actress Margot Kidder states:

> Abortion might be killing a life; I don't know. That to me is not an issue. If there is a sin, it is the sin that we adults perpetrate on the children of the earth who truly are innocent and defenseless by bringing those children into the world when they will not be cared for . . . I'm not pro abortion . . . because abortion hurts. It's emotionally painful. I am pro *choice*—that being the choice of the mother, choice over my own body—because ultimately it's my womb, my nine months and the child I have to nurture.[3]

Despite her recognition of the fact that abortion might be killing an innocent and defenseless life and that abortion hurts and is emotionally painful, Ms. Kidder will not allow these grave concerns to deter her from a self-centered approach to life demonstrated by her choice of words— *"my own body . . . my* nine months . . . the child *I* have to nurture." I fear that this studied approach to the destruction of another life is a reflection of values being imposed upon the average American citizen through the media, the entertainment industry, and public policy.

The womb was designed to be a sanctuary in which a child could grow, and the taking of a baby's life while in that sanctuary is nothing short of manslaughter. How far our nation has strayed from our prized principles of life and liberty for all! As long as abortions are performed, some people will never enjoy even the first of these principles.

As Archibald Cox once said, "The opinion [*Roe v. Wade*] fails even to consider what I would suppose to be the most compelling interest of the state in prohibiting abortion: the interest in maintaining that respect for the paramount sanctity of human life which has always been at the center of Western civilization."[4]

When a nation endorses abortion it is telling its citizens that life is cheap. All over America societies are founded to prevent cruelty to animals, to save the whales, to stop medical testing on cats, and to stop the needless destruction of trees. These are all fine and good, but we must wonder if something is out of balance when the very people who advocate such benevolent programs zealously promote the "right" to kill our own offspring. Are they blind to the fact that they are committing *the ultimate in child abuse* while adding humans to the list of "endangered species"? It is time we stopped polluting our moral environment and did something to reverse the foul trend of rampant abortion.

PRO-CHOICE BLIND SPOTS

It appears that feminists, the vast majority of whom ardently support abortion rights, are blinded to the fact that promiscuous men favor abortion because it is a convenient escape route to avoid reaping what they have sown. "Feminists need to ask why the 'sexist' establishment supports abortion," says one commentator. "It may be that abortion enhances the male's freedom to exploit by sparing him from the worry of paternity."[5]

Women must recognize that even though they have historically been exploited, they do not have license to exploit others, namely, their unborn babies. Many of us learned as children that two wrongs do not make a right. Abortion is the ultimate wrong.

Abortion advocates have argued for years that if women are free to choose whether or not to have babies, the child abuse rate will decrease. That is absolutely false. On the contrary, statistics show that child abuse cases increased *500 percent* in the ten years following the legalization of abortion in the United States. And as victims of abortion, the ultimate child abuse, each year over a million and a half innocent children are denied the right to life, while their mothers exercise the right to kill.

No matter how you look at it or try to excuse it, abortion is wrong. But "wrong" is taken a step farther out of moral bounds when abortion is performed on minors with neither the consent or knowledge of the young girls' parents.

At our 1991 national convention, CWA member Eileen Roberts related the story of her teenage daughter's abortion, which was lawfully performed without her knowledge. The abortionist performed the procedure without knowledge of the young girl's medical history—which in this case contained vital information—because the "confidential" nature of the abortion prevented him from consulting the girl's parents. It wasn't until complications arose that Eileen was even notified of her daughter's abortion.

"All I am saying is that we, as parents, have the right to know!" Eileen explained. Mr. and Mrs. Roberts certainly do have the right to know if their daughter is being counseled to have an abortion. There is an irreconcilable inconsistency between the fact that parents must personally authorize schools to give their children prescribed medication, but are denied the right to know if their daughter is pursuing a surgical operation! Parental influence and involvement is being consistently undercut by an ever-growing government. This is not what women desire for their children, and it diminishes their role in motherhood.

What about unplanned pregnancies? What can we do to help women and girls who do not feel capable of bearing or raising a child? In addition to local congregations who offer assistance to mothers in unplanned pregnancies, there are over three thousand crisis pregnancy centers located throughout the nation. Crisis pregnancy centers vary according to local needs and capabilities, but among the services and items they provide to pregnant women are housing; supplies, such as maternity and baby clothing, bottles, diapers, and formula; programs to assist women in finishing high school and finding employment; and a program known as PACE (Post-Abortion Counseling and Education) for women suffering from the trauma of abortion.

Bethany Christian Services, the largest nonprofit pregnancy counseling agency in the United States, provides a similar but distinct service in its effort to help women make a choice that is best for both the mothers and their babies. They counsel pregnant women about parenting, marriage, and/or making an adoption plan for the baby. All of their services are offered at no cost to pregnant women, and adoptions are offered at only half the normal cost to adopting parents. Where would these women turn if it were not for the loving care of the pro-life community?

MOTHERS WHO ARE ALONE
Abortion is not the only social evil that assaults motherhood. Divorce and promiscuity have both made mother-

hood far more difficult by leaving millions of mothers to rear their children with no help from the father.

In 1992, Vice President Dan Quayle touched off a furor in Hollywood and around the country when he made his famous reference to the television character Murphy Brown, implying that the television show undermined family values. Far from criticizing single mothers, Vice President Quayle was making the point that Hollywood's glamorization of irresponsibility in fathers is a disgrace and a disservice to our nation.

The vice president's point hit home. As news commentator Mona Charen notes:

> The breakdown of the family isn't just one issue among many to which politicians must pay lip service. It is the crux, the cause, and the origin of most social and economic woes in this society. . . . For blacks and whites alike, it is the family structure that is the greatest determinant of wealth, health and order. Poverty, crime and illness are worse among blacks, because family disintegration is more pronounced. According to the American Humane Association, roughly 25 percent of child abuse cases occur in single, female-headed households. . . . Intact families are not an "ideal," nor are they a throwback to less enlightened times. Intact families are an urgent social, political and economic necessity. Any public policy that overlooks that truth is missing the whole story.

Fortune magazine devoted its August 1992 issue to the question of our nation's children. The issue was aptly titled "Children in Crisis." These are among the alarming statistics given regarding children raised in single-parent homes:

- Children from single-parent homes are 100 to 200 percent more likely than children from two-parent families to have emotional and behavioral problems;

- Children from single-parent homes are 50 percent more likely to have learning disabilities than children from two-parent families;
- Over 80 percent of adolescents admitted for psychiatric reasons in our nation's hospitals come from single-parent homes;
- Three-quarters of the children of single parents will live in poverty during at least part of the crucial first ten years of their lives;
- The most reliable predictor of crime is neither poverty nor race but growing up fatherless.

Single motherhood is a far cry from freedom or liberation. Being a parent is a strenuous undertaking even when the duty is shared with a spouse; how much harder it is to do alone! Even apart from the great demands on the single parent are the detrimental effects of single parenting on children.

Not only is single motherhood emotionally taxing; it also involves an extreme financial burden. According to Census Bureau data, single-parent homes are five times as likely to be poor as two-parent families.

Contrary to modern myths, fathers are not just another disposable item in the nursery. Responsible fathers are vital to the well-being of all societies. A caring mother wants to have a loving father in the home, but tragically, this is not always possible. Nearly a quarter of today's youth live in single-parent families, over two and a half times as many as did in 1960. For blacks during this period, the rate jumped from over 21 percent to over 54 percent.[7]

If you are a single mother, you already know how difficult the road can be. You are not walking it alone, however. God has promised to be a father to your children. "A father to the fatherless, a defender of widows, is God in his holy dwelling. God sets the lonely in families, he leads forth the prisoners with singing; but the rebellious live in a sun-scorched land" (Psalm 68:5-6). God will keep you in his care and support you with his might.

THE VALUE OF MOTHERING

Consider the fortunate woman who has a loving husband who is a good father. Her family may not be rich or even middle class, but by making sacrifices they are able to get by on one income. This woman has chosen to stay home and fill the traditional role of mother. She believes she is doing right, but with the influence in today's society she may feel uncomfortable.

She doesn't have the flashy trappings of a career, and she may feel almost ashamed when she introduces herself to a newcomer: "Oh, I'm just a housewife." She feels inferior because she's not computer-literate, her calendar is empty of dates for power lunches, and her most important papers are the crayon scribblings on the refrigerator door. If she can overcome those self-imposed attitudes, she can enjoy the contentment and satisfaction that comes as her children develop and mature.

Most feminists consider the traditional, stay-at-home mother worthless and unproductive. The woman who chooses to place child rearing and homemaking above a career will find no encouragement in the mass media. Many of her friends will work full-time as well, so she may become isolated and feel resentful. If she's a churchgoer, she may receive little support from the church. The truth is, too many church women have also decided to find "fulfillment" outside the home.

After I spoke at a women's conference in the Midwest, a young, attractive lady with two young daughters waited to speak to me. I couldn't help noticing her two little blonde girls, for they looked as if they had stepped out of a magazine ad.

Her first words to me were, "Mrs. LaHaye, I don't feel like I'm fulfilling my potential in life."

This woman was overlooking the fact that developing good character traits in two lovely daughters was the greatest challenge she could have at this stage of her life. Her question to me should have been, "How can I give my daughters the best moral training when there are so many forces working against me?"

THE MOTHER-CHILD BOND

In her book *Home by Choice: Facing the Effects of Mother's Absence: Creating Emotional Security in Children*, Dr. Brenda Hunter voices the opinion of a majority of scholars on the question of a child's need for sustained parental involvement. "Increasingly," Dr. Hunter writes, "child development experts are saying what many mothers and fathers have known all along—that to be fully human a child needs to be intensely loved and cared for by someone who won't 'pack up and leave at five o'clock.' "[8]

Dr. Hunter gives a persuasive argument for the contention that secure attachment is the key to emotional health:

Any woman who gives her child the love and nurture every child needs is giving him a priceless gift. She is shaping her child's self-concept and teaching him lessons about love and intimacy that last a lifetime.

In his 1969 book *Attachment*, British psychiatrist John Bowlby wrote about the centrality of the baby's emotional bond or attachment to his mother, which Bowlby believes is the "foundation stone of personality." Bowlby states that "the young child's hunger for his mother's love and presence is as great as his hunger for food" and that her loss or absence "inevitably generates a powerful sense of loss and anger."[9]

The old saying "Absence makes the heart grow fonder" is not true when applied to a child's relationship with his parents. On the contrary, "absence generates profound feelings of rejection and a yearning for love that can dominate the whole of life," says Dr. Hunter. "Harvard psychiatrist Armand Nicholi says that those individuals who suffer from severe nonorganic emotional illness have one thing in common: all have experienced the 'absence of a parent through death, divorce, a time demanding job or other reasons.' "[10]

Feminist actress-activist-aerobicist Jane Fonda has either rethought aspects of her position on women's liberation or is blind beyond belief to the inconsistencies presented by the following statement: "When you see what's happening to kids," Fonda told a *USA Today* reporter, "you can't help but think that somebody should have been at home, minding the kids."[11]

Not all feminists share Fonda's observation; many still deny the importance of having a mother at home. But Dr. Hunter observes that it is a woman's relationship with her parents that may affect her desire to have children, her feelings about feminism, her investment in her career versus the mothering role, as well as her level of maternal separation anxiety. She notes that famous feminists such as Betty Friedan, Germaine Greer, and Gloria Steinem all suffered from a lack of parental love, citing evidence for her conclusions.

While it is not my purpose to attack these prominent feminists on a personal level, I do think it is important that we see that yesterday's victims are very often today's victimizers. Dr. Hunter asks:

> Who would not feel sympathy for a woman who has looked at parental rejection with such rigor? Yet I am angry that these women used their impressive intel-

lects to shape social policy without first examining and understanding their own personal histories. A whole generation of women has marched to their misguided anti-marriage, anti-male, and anti-family music. Yet it is ultimately our own fault to have been so thoroughly influenced by feminist rhetoric without first looking at the origins of this rage.[12]

OUR NATION NEEDS STRONG FAMILIES

"The most important family value is: when a woman has a baby, let her stay home to bond properly with the child," says Yale psychologist Edward Zigler. "That determines the future."[13] Writing for *Fortune* magazine, Louis Richman noted that the destiny of our nation is in critical and grave condition:

> If the well-being of its children is the proper measure of the health of a civilization, the United States is in grave danger. . . . The bipartisan national Commission on Children wrote in "Beyond Rhetoric," its 1991 report, that addressing the unmet needs of American youngsters "is a national imperative as compelling as an armed attack or a natural disaster."[14]

Why is it that the truly important rarely strikes us as being urgent? In the nineties, the ten years Concerned Women for America has called the "decade of destiny" for America's children, contemporary American culture is its own worst enemy. We know no culture can long survive without strong families. The sexual permissiveness and cavalier view of the traditional family, adopted by our culture, spell disaster for our nation. It is clear that we can no longer depend on our government and media to promote the values we embrace.

What can we do to preserve our motherhood and our

children? Those of us who desire to train our children apart from government control must take a proactive stance, aggressively working to protect our families. The Bible admonishes us: "Be sure you know the condition of your flocks, give careful attention to your herds; for riches do not endure forever, and a crown is not secure for all generations" (Proverbs 27:23-24). Women want to be good mothers, and it is time we aggressively act on our desires.

With the liberal voices urging parents to send their children to school at a younger and younger age (thus giving them ample opportunity to inculcate their worldly and godless philosophies), Christian parents have less and less time to impart wisdom and faith to their children. Thus an important time for parent-child bonding is being taken by the government-controlled schools. This devastating trend is being recognized and bemoaned even by some in the secular media:

> Families are the institution in which character is formed, and what kinds of characters are being forged, what kinds of citizens are being molded to carry on our society, when our principal socializing institution has had so much parental time withdrawn from it and so many Americans bear such scars from what has happened in their families? The answer is dismayingly clear for dysfunctional underclass families, whose children so often turn out flagrantly antisocial, with such high rates of delinquency and criminality.[15]

Even if we come from dysfunctional families, we must not simply submit to defeat. Rather, we need to do everything possible to restore the well-being of our homes. The first place to turn is to biblical guidance. Your local church may have a support group that would be a great place to start, but be sure the teachings of the group are based on God's Word.

Second, we need to realize that as mothers, our duty is not merely to provide for the physical needs of our children, but to impart truths that will instruct and equip them for the duration of their lives. Children are like wet cement; early impressions made on them are long lasting. Abdication of our role as mothers or the adoption of a haphazard approach will only cheat our children. God has called us to do more:

> Hear, O Israel: The LORD our God, the LORD is one. Love the LORD your God with all your heart and with all your soul and with all your strength. These commandments that I give you today are to be upon your hearts. Impress them on your children. Talk about them when you sit at home and when you walk along the road, when you lie down, and when you get up. (Deuteronomy 6:4-7)

WHY PARENTS ARE THE BEST EDUCATORS

If we do not teach our children the things God has commanded, there are many out there who would be more than willing to take over our role. The education establishment has been pressing for control of our children's minds at younger and younger ages. Naive parents will praise our public educators for their diligence and apparent deep concern for the welfare of our children. Unfortunately, however, the underlying motive of the educational elite may be nothing short of socialization according to an amoral, godless standard.

When you hear people pushing child care as the best place for preschool children, beware! A hidden agenda lurks behind social parenting. The mere fact that feminists push for universal child care should signal danger. The

National Organization for Women has been pushing it since the late sixties, and the Children's Defense Fund since the late seventies, but child care and social parenting have been part of the feminist agenda for decades.

In her book *Can Motherhood Survive: A Christian Looks at Social Parenting,* Connie Marshner sounds the trumpet against the national industry of day care, which she sees as "opening the wedge of the campaign for social parenting."[16]

> Social parenting includes, for instance, the attitude that it is the school's responsibility to provide children with medical care and psychological intervention. It also includes the notion that it is society's obligation to remove the children of the poor from parental influence. Look around and you'll see lots of examples of the idea that "we" can raise kids better than parents can, "we" usually being professionally credentialed members of the so-called "helping professions."[17]

Thomas Sowell, an economist and a senior fellow at the Hoover Institution, has made this noteworthy observation: "One of the first things a family tries to teach its children is the difference between right and wrong. One of the first things our schools try to destroy is that distinction."[18]

Why do our public schools work to undermine our children's faith? Why is there such confusion and such a crisis of values in American culture? Contemporary theologian R. C. Sproul had this answer:

> The confusion of ideas and viewpoints became a national crisis when the Supreme Court ruled on the volatile issue of prayer in the public schools. The basic principle in view was that a religious view of life should not be imposed on the people by the state in a public schoolroom. . . . To teach children about life and the

world in which they live without reference to God is to make a statement about God. It screams a statement. The message is either that there is no God or that God is irrelevant. Either is the same as no God at all.[19]

The National Education Association, a radical union that wields great political clout, has an aggressively pro-homosexual agenda for our children. One example of how this agenda was being worked out in 1992 is the New York City public school's first-grade teacher's guide, which suggested the reading of two aggressively pro-homosexual books in their curriculum. The first of these, *Heather Has Two Mommies,* is the story of a lesbian couple having a child through artificial insemination. The other, *Daddy's Roommate,* features a happy child with two male parents who concludes that being "gay" is yet one more kind of love. John Leo, writing for *The Washington Times,* notes:

> These are not books about tolerance—letting people alone and not picking on others because of sexual orientation or family structure. They are books celebrating the wonders of double-mommy and double-daddy households. But surely schools can generate respect for Catholic children, let's say, without putting "Heather Finds Peace as a Nun" on the reading list. . . . So how did these books make it onto the reading list?
> The answer is tucked away on page 145 of the city's "Children of the Rainbow" first-grade curriculum: Teachers must "be aware of varied family structures— including gay or lesbian parents," and "Children must be taught to acknowledge the positive aspects of each type of household."[20]

John Leo then cites a letter written in response to the first-grade curriculum's objective of teaching that homosexuality is amorally acceptable practice. "If my wife and I choose to believe in what the Holy Scriptures say about homosexuality," quotes Leo, "it is not up to teachers, or any municipal or political group, public or private, to refute these teachings."[21]

NEEDED: FIRM MORAL TEACHING

On this same subject, another journalist, Richard Vigilante, observes that the proponents of the pro-homosexuality message do not practice the tolerance they expect of Christians. Far from it, they disregard the distress of concerned parents who do not relish their attempts to market homosexuality. As Vigilante observes, it "is not tolerance but moral and intellectual imperialism"[22] that the pro-homosexual lobbyists promote. He makes another insightful comment: "If Americans do not have the right to maintain, for themselves and their families, moral beliefs taught for millennia by the religions to which between 70 and 90 percent of the population subscribe, then a lot of us are living in the wrong country."[23]

I certainly hope I'm not living in the wrong country, but I have to admit the moral climate here is degenerating at a rapid pace. One thing we must do is redeem the time because the days are evil (Ephesians 5:16). While we have the opportunity, we must teach our children to do good. Parents are instructed by God to teach their child to respect authority, instruct him to be obedient, turn him away from evil toward Jesus Christ, train him according to the way God designed him, and lead him from the beginning to develop character traits that will prepare him for marriage. If we mothers do our part, God promises that our child will not depart from our teaching when he or she reaches maturity (Proverbs 22:6).

Mothers desire to raise children who will not be promiscuous and put their lives at risk, but today we are faced head-on with the problem of teenage sex and pregnancy. Feminists and other liberal groups love to argue that teens are "going to have sex, anyway," so we need to equip them with knowledge and birth control. It *is* important that we teach our children about their sexuality and all the changes that occur in their growing bodies, but it is critical that we teach our children to respect their sexuality and not throw the priceless gift of virginity away in the name of raging hormones. This education needs to take place within the family, with parents taking responsibility over their children.

I firmly believe that most teenage girls do not desire to have sex but feel pressured, whether by boyfriends or other peers, that this is expected of them to be "cool." Ironically, in a study authored by a Planned Parenthood affiliate, Family Planning Perspectives, over one thousand sexually active girls age sixteen or younger were asked what topic they wanted more information on. Eighty-four percent of them responded that they wanted to know "how to say no without hurting the other person's feelings." It seems clear to me that teenage girls are crying out for help, but the only thing they hear is that it is all right to have sex and they should "follow their feelings."[24] Instead of responding to their cry for help, we hand them a condom and then deceive them by saying this will give them safe sex.

According to the Department of Health and Human Services, the birthrate of unmarried teens has increased almost five and a half times since 1940 with half of the increase occurring since 1975. So, for all the praise and recognition liberal thinking has received, it appears that the increasing availability of birth control, the legalization of abortion, widespread sex education, and the threat of AIDS and other diseases have done nothing to slow the growth of teen pregnancy.

Mothers, we need to look at this seriously. Our children need to be taught that God created sexual intercourse solely for marriage, and no school or interest group will teach them about sex and how to respect it like you can. No one has the interest in our sons or daughters like we do, and we must not let the opportunity slip through our fingers.

THE BEAUTY OF MOTHERHOOD

God longs for us to know life, not mere existence. He longs for us to know the beauty of motherhood, not merely the hard work and inevitable pain.

Our society has experimented enough on children, and today we are reaping the tares sown in the sixties. Licensed promiscuity has brought us AIDS, rampant venereal disease, abortion, heartbreak, divorce, and poverty. The feminist drive to boot women out of the homes and into the workplace has left our nation's children out in the cold. What have we learned from our massive experiment? That God's way was right after all. Myron Magnet writes:

> Now we need to reflect on what we've learned, that children are important, that they don't grow up well unless we bring them up, that they need two parents, that our needs can't shoulder theirs aside, that commitments and responsibilities to others have to take precedence over personal gratification, that nothing is more gratifying than to see children flourish.[25]

Women want to experience the beauty of motherhood. We want to restore mothers to their place of honor, for in doing so we will affirm and value our children and our families. We will also find the joy, honor, and fulfillment in motherhood that God intended.

Part of the beauty of motherhood is knowing that we are successful in our training, and success comes from teaching our children the right things in the right way at the right time. As mothers, we should not try to be our children's "buddy" or "one of the kids," but we are to be counselors, authorities, and loving disciplinarians.

We know that with motherhood comes pain, but in pain there is beauty. We grow when we grieve, and God uses even pain-filled times to teach us and bring us into a greater understanding of our responsibilities to our children. So we don't ask for trouble-free roads as we mother children, but we do ask that society stop hampering our efforts to see our children mature in godliness. God has given them to us for such a short time, and we want to be excellent stewards of these treasures. We live for the day when our grown children rise up and call us "blessed."

ORGANIZATIONS SUPPORTING MOTHERHOOD

The following is a list of organizations whose objective is to support the family. For more information on these organizations, write them at the addresses given.

- Christian Action Council (101 W. Broad Street, Suite 500, Falls Church, VA 22046) seeks through both tangible and intangible means to demonstrate the love of God to women in crisis and to show them that they are precious in his sight. As a part of this program, CAC operates 450 crisis pregnancy centers throughout the nation.
- Home by Choice (P.O. Box 103, Vienna, VA 22180) has as its objective to provide full-time mothers encouraging fellowship, intellectual stimulation, and spiritual growth.
- Mothers at Home (P.O. Box 2209, Merrifield, VA 22116) strives to reinforce women's choice of full-time motherhood.
- Moms in Touch (P.O. Box 1163, Poway, CA 92064) encourages the formation of small groups devoted to prayer for children, children's schools, teachers, and administrators.

- Mothers of Pre-Schoolers (MOPS International, 4175 Harlan Street, #105, Wheat Ridge, CO 80033) holds regular group meetings with biblical instruction relating to womanhood, marriage, child rearing, and family relationships.
- Cottage Connections (11113 Radison Court, Burnsville, MN 55337) is a networking effort among Christian homemakers that supports women by sharing thoughts and concerns in a newsletter.
- Gentle Spirit (c/o Cheryl Lindsey, 3108 90th Avenue East, Puyallup, WA 98371) is dedicated to helping women obey Titus 2:4-5 and 1 Peter 3:4.
- Formerly Employed Mothers at the Leading Edge (FEMALE, P.O. Box 31, Elmhurst, IL 60126) is a support advocacy group for mothers who have chosen to stay home for a time to raise their children. They have a nationwide network of local support chapters.

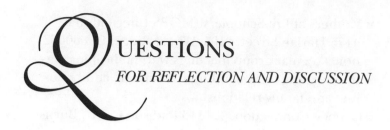

QUESTIONS
FOR REFLECTION AND DISCUSSION

1. What can the Christian community do to assist women in unplanned pregnancies?
2. How can we work to provide children a healthy environment in which to grow up?
3. How essential are two parents to a child's well-being?
4. Does absence really make the heart grow fonder when it comes to a child and his parents?
5. What are a parent's responsibilities before God?
6. Why do children need to be trained to do what's right?
7. How can the beauty of motherhood be restored in our society?
8. What goals should a mother have for her children?

DESIRES
IN
OUR
WORLD

8

We Want Joy and Satisfaction in Our Work

Regardless of a woman's status in life, she will need to work. Work is the force that drives us to grow and be and do. Whether you work at home as a homemaker, from home in some sort of business, or in the rapidly expanding workplace, work will be an important part of your life. As Booker T. Washington said, "Nothing ever comes to one, that is worth having, except as a result of hard work."[1] We expend our energies and work at the things and relationships that are important to us. God gave Adam work even in the Garden of Eden before the Fall, and naming those animals and tending the Garden weren't easy tasks! God designed us with a desire and drive to *do* something with our lives.

In today's economy, you may be required to find work that compensates your time financially. In other words, you need a job that pays well enough to balance your increased expenses as you enter the workplace. Perhaps you have been left to support yourself because of the death of your spouse or a broken marriage, or perhaps you have expenses that your husband's income will not cover. Whether you work out of necessity or for self-expression and personal

development, you want your work to be both financially
rewarding and personally satisfying.

Contrary to the feminist view, professional employment is
not more fulfilling or significant than working in the home
or in other spheres. Nor is work intended to be, as feminists
contend, an arena for competition against men. The implied
promise that professional supremacy over men empowers
and satisfies women is a hoax. Sadly, professional success is
often achieved at the expense of personal satisfaction.

> When there is no private realm, rank derives only from
> jobs, and a person without a job, no matter how charm-
> ing, amusing, educated, beautiful, or rich, is a person
> without social identification or standing. That is why
> women who were once proud of singlehandedly main-
> taining private, domestic, community, social, and cul-
> tural life for men who could manage only one job
> apiece, are now ashamed or defensive about being
> housewives.—Judith Martin[2]

It is important for women to hold on to the "private
realm" Judith Martin describes, but necessary employment
outside the home has become a reluctant reality for many
women. The 1990 Roper poll for Virginia Slims confirms
that most women today prefer staying at home to working
outside the home. Specifically, 51 percent of all women and
55 percent of married women would prefer to stay home.
The career conflict is particularly poignant for the mothers
of young children. Seventy-three percent of the respon-
dents in a 1990 Gallup poll for the Los Angeles Times Syndi-
cate think that children today are better off with a mother
who is not employed outside the home. While the majority
of Americans recognize the importance of having mother
at home for her children, some women are fighting vigor-
ously for a woman's right to make her career her priority, to

work long hours, and to achieve great status in the eyes of the world; in essence, to imitate men.

WHAT GOD REQUIRES OF OUR WORK: EXCELLENCE AND DILIGENCE

Whether we work at home or in the professional work force, we need to find a purpose for our work. What should our goals be? God's Word gives us an answer: "A good name is more desirable than great riches; to be esteemed is better than silver or gold. . . . Do you see a man skilled in his work? He will serve before kings; he will not serve before obscure men" (Proverbs 22:1, 29).

What a challenge those verses present to us! We are to earn good names for ourselves in our work; we are to work with skill and excellence. Excellence means being of the highest or finest quality, exceptionally good. Too often we fall short of excellence in our work. In Colossians 3:22 God says we are to be obedient to our employers and work with sincerity. In other words, we are told to pursue excellence in our reputations, in our work, and in whatever we do: "Whatever you do, work at it with all your heart, as working for the Lord, not for men, since you know that you will receive an inheritance from the Lord as a reward. It is the Lord Christ you are serving" (Colossians 3:23-24).

Christians ought to be known not only for the excellence of their work, but also for their diligence. When Christians do not work diligently, this reflects poorly upon God, our Father. Paul reminded the Thessalonians of the importance of work: "We hear that some among you are idle. They are not busy; they are busybodies. Such people we command and urge in the Lord Jesus Christ to settle down and earn the bread they eat. And as for you, brothers, never tire of doing what is right" (2 Thessalonians 3:11-13).

Paul even went so far as to say, "If anyone does not provide for his relatives, and especially for his immediate family, he has denied the faith and is worse than an unbeliever" (1 Timothy 5:8). Clearly, work is not an option. God honors hard workers. We know this from his own example. Proverbs 18:9 tells us that "one who is slack in his work is brother to one who destroys." Obviously, whatever work you are engaged in, God expects you to perform it to the best of your ability.

MOTHERHOOD IS MEANINGFUL EMPLOYMENT

Most women do work, and there is no harder or more meaningful work than a mother's work with her children. I firmly believe that if a woman has young children, her obvious first choice should be to stay at home with them. Unfortunately, many mothers today, both married and single, are finding themselves in an economic position that requires them to work simply to make ends meet. Eighty-eight percent of women responding to a 1987 survey of eight hundred women agreed with this statement: "If I could afford it, I would rather be at home with my children."

Our high standard of living, expanding medical costs, and the excessive tax burden are all responsible for many families' inability to support themselves on husbands' income alone. But despite financial sacrifices that may be required, if it is at all possible, I believe it critical to the future of her children that a mother stay at home with them, especially during their preschool years.

Studies show that most children who get into trouble do so because of a lack of parental supervision and involvement in their lives at crucial times. The critical bonding between parents and children takes place early in a child's life and builds the emotional foundation for the child's future social relationships. Beyond that initial bonding, however, there is a tremendous need for children to have someone waiting when they come home. The mere existence of the latchkey child is a sad commentary on the place to which we have relegated our children in our supposedly enlightened society.

> A study done in April by the American Academy of
> Pediatrics showed that latchkey children were more
> socially isolated than other children. . . . The study
> also showed that children in the care of older brothers
> or sisters ranked themselves lower in self-worth, social
> acceptance, and physical appearance. Other studies by
> the academy indicate that latchkey kids were about
> twice as likely as supervised children to smoke, drink
> alcohol, and use marijuana.[3]

It is clear that children do not gravitate toward good activities during unsupervised time. They need the involvement of alert adults in their lives. But even when adults are supervising children's time, there are inevitable repercussions to compromising the biblical example of a mother being intimately involved in the lives of her children. Children fare better when *their parents,* not baby-sitters or siblings, give them attention and concern.

Secular observers share this view: "Family care, day care centers, self-care," writes Susan Caminiti in *Fortune* magazine, "it comes down to a lot of not-quite-satisfying choices for parents who want to do their best for their kids but can't be home when their children aren't in school. . . . But nothing will change the hard, basic principle of child care, sometimes forgotten: *The kids' welfare comes first, and vigilant parents are its best protector.*"[4]

While there are many instances in which the mother must work to support her family, especially in the case of single mothers who do not receive financial support, I would like to challenge women who work simply for secondary reasons—a vacation, a second car, intellectual stimulation, the opportunity to be with peers, or the pursuit of significance through professional development. Are you keeping your children's best interests in mind? Who else but you will prize your children, uphold them, seek their best, develop the character traits you want for them, and provide the loving support they need? Don't expect their teachers to take on that role. It is yours.

Is it any wonder that our society is plummeting morally and socially when such a large percentage of children must return to an empty house following a day filled with the pressure of peers and school? Is it any wonder that our nation's children are faring increasingly worse academically (SAT scores are at their lowest in thirty years) and psychologically (teen homicide and suicide rates have escalated dramatically), and that our crime rate is at an all-time high?

Children, like gardens, require tending. Weeds grow more quickly and tenaciously than the seedlings we purposely plant. Parents are called to tend their children as a conscientious farmer tends the fruit of his soil. When parent substitutes are assigned the role of parenting children, the consequences are grave, particularly in the first few years of a child's life.

"The cost of separation in early childhood is high," writes Dr. Brenda Hunter. "The evidence since 1980 indicates that when a baby is placed in substitute care, even good quality care such as nanny care, for twenty or more hours per week during his first year of life, he is at risk psychologically."[5]

Not everyone prizes the work and effort that homemaking and child rearing require. "For a woman to get a rewarding sense of total creation by way of the multiple monotonous chores that are her daily lot would be as irrational as for an assembly line worker to rejoice that he had created an automobile because he tightened a bolt," wrote Edith Mendel Stern in 1949.[6]

Despite those who view child rearing as mindless and monotonous, if a woman chooses to stay at home to be with her children, she has not chosen to squander her talents and education. There is abundant opportunity for the employment and cultivation of these in her work at home. The work of an excellent housewife and mother is anything but negligible or frivolous. She hardly fritters her time away watching the "soaps," as some seem to think. Although she may not bring home a paycheck at the end of the week, her work has material worth as well as emotional and spiritual value beyond measure.

"What's a mother worth?" asks Dr. Hunter. "About $25,000 a year. Roles: nursemaid, housekeeper, dishwasher, laundress, food buyer, chauffeur, gardener, maintenance person, seamstress, dietitian, practical nurse, coach, teacher, interior decorator, religious education instructor, and child psychologist, to name a few."[7]

"To be a housewife is . . . a difficult, a wrenching, sometimes an ungrateful job if it is looked on only as a job," writes Phyllis McGinley. "Regarded as a profession, it is the noblest. . . . Let none persuade us differently or the world is lost indeed."[8]

A mother's presence in her children's lives as friend and teacher is of great significance, for it will produce rewards that outlive the span of her years. What work outside the home could compete with cultivating the supremely important legacy of God-fearing children? When we choose material things over the higher good of our children's well-being, we are tacitly teaching them to value things over people. Our children are not the only sad victims of this choice; society suffers as well. But when we put people before possessions in our hearts, we are sowing seeds of enduring satisfaction. "At the end of your life," says former First Lady Barbara Bush, "you will never regret not having passed one more test, not winning one more verdict, or not closing one more deal. You will regret time not spent with a husband, friend, a child or a parent."[9]

Our society must learn that we will get what we pay for. There simply are no shortcuts to raising prosperous, happy children. I believe that many of the problems we are facing on school campuses—gun fights, knives, drugs, and alcohol—are simply the outward expression of angry young people who have been frustrated by their attempts to find intimacy and control at home.

I do recognize that in our society there are imperfect conditions we all must face and attempt to overcome. Many women work as they do only because it is necessary. When life is not ideal, we must make the most of what we have.

EMPLOYMENT OPTIONS

Many mothers wish they had the option of not working professionally in order to be able to stay at home with their children, but they do not have such a luxury. Fortunately, several alternatives to regular full-time employment are becoming more and more common. These include part-time employment, flex time, compressed work weeks, job sharing, home-based work, and split-shift parenting.

Progressive companies are recognizing the need to provide benefits and flexible arrangements to an increasing number of employees whose life-styles reflect the demands of a changing world. Technological advances such as the fax machine and modems also can be used to the advantage of women wanting to stay home but needing to make an income. The combination of creativity, initiative, and skill can go a long way in the professional world.

Government-enforced parental leave, a program designed to provide job security to women who seek extended periods of time away from work to tend to family-related needs, may, in fact, have the reverse effect. Employers will no doubt think twice about hiring a prospective female employee of childbearing age for fear that she will suddenly leave to have babies, thus creating an awkward and costly situation for the employer, who may need to find a long-term temporary replacement during the woman's absence.

TAKING TIME FOR THE "MOMMY TRACK"

The phrase "mommy track" has become popular in recent years as professional women have begun to shift their priorities and take time out for motherhood. Many women are opting to drop out of the professional world to be with their children during the early formative years of their children's lives.

These women have come to the realization that they will never be able to turn back the clock and return to their children's earliest years. So, seizing the moment, they have put their children above their careers without discarding their profession entirely.

Women on the "mommy track" no longer believe in Superwoman. They have come to grips with the fact that the unexamined life is not worth living; specifically, that their lives require constant evaluation and prioritization. They have realized that some decisions in life involve sacrifice. It is very likely that a woman deferring her career in order to nurture her children will experience professional setbacks.

Is this wrong or unfair? I don't think so.

"Is it fair that women who take long maternity leaves or work only part time to be with their kids should lose ground at work?" asks Nancy J. Perry in *Fortune* magazine. "Most executives—male and female—don't see any other alternative."[10] Kathleen Cooper, Exxon Corporation's chief economist, observes: "We think of missing the development of a child. But the employer is thinking the same things about his employee. I don't think that's wrong. Treating everyone equally is unfair to the woman who stays and puts in the hours."[11]

WORKING AGAINST WOMEN:
DISCRIMINATION AND AFFIRMATIVE ACTION

Are women the victims of professional discrimination? Some fear that women in corporate America are a generation away from real success because of discrimination. Such prejudice against women based on gender rather than performance ought to be eliminated. Indeed, legally it has been. The federal Equal Employment Opportunity Act of 1972 applies to hiring, pay, and promotion. Discrimination against women in the workplace is against federal law.

Though the law serves as our guide, it does not change hearts overnight. I do not believe that we can legislate a change of heart on the part of male employers. If we truly want discrimination eradicated, we must change the hearts and minds of those who discriminate.

I think we would all agree that women deserve to be regarded with respect in the professional world and judged, not by gender, but by performance. I believe there are many instances in which a woman is the best applicant for the job. For example, I feel uniquely qualified to serve as the president of Concerned Women for America. For many reasons, a man would be less effective in my position.

Statistics, however, indicate that a woman earns about seventy-four cents to every dollar a man makes. The wage gap is due in part to the different occupations men and women often hold. Figured into these statistics also are the facts that more women work part-time and that their length of service is often shorter. Both facts are just cause for a lower income.

But there is also another dimension to this disparity. Some call it the gender-based wage gap—paying a man more than a woman for the same job. Such a regrettable practice is a feminist byword. Feminists have a legitimate point when they find fault with one person being paid more than another for the same performance, unless the pay disparity reflects differing financial needs. For example, if one person must support a family, while another person in the same position supports no one but himself or herself, I think the employer has every right to compensate the head-of-household employee accordingly. This would be true, of course, whether the needier employee was male or female.

Paying employees according to family needs is certainly the exception, not the rule, in America today. One company that has this policy is Custom Shutters in Como, Texas. Its president, Bill C. Watts, explains how the policy works in his company:

> Our policy seeks to pay according to what we perceive to be the need in a family with children under 16 years of age with only one wage earner. It may be the male or the female that is the wage earner, so we don't discriminate, but simply pay more to those who have one or more children in the family at home: a wage supplement of $1 per hour [for a head of household in a single-income family] plus $.75 per hour for each child under 16 in the family. We pick out the children in the family because they are an added expense, and we want to encourage one or the other parent to be at home. . . . We believe that one of the parents should be at home with the child, so we put our money where our belief is.[12]

While it is disheartening to discover the frequency of the gender-based wage gap, and even more disheartening to be a victim of it, government ought not to legislate specifics in the realm of salary equity. At a Heritage Foundation lecture given in November of 1992, Dr. Deborah Walker, Bradley scholar at the Heritage Foundation (through June 1993) maintained that the coercive hand of government actually

worsens gender-based difficulties. Cultural change, Dr.
Walker affirmed, ought to take place under the principles
of self-ownership, private property, and individual liberty.
"These are, after all, the principles upon which our government was founded," she explained. "Without them, can we
truly call ourselves a free society?"

It has been argued that in a competitive market, pay ineq-
uities will naturally work their way out of the system. Free
markets lead to free choice and create a stronger economy.
A stronger economy affords women the choice not to enter
the work force at all. And isn't choice what feminists say
they are after?

Women are not second-class citizens and do not appreciate being treated as such anywhere, whether in the home,
at work, or at church. In many instances, the performance
of women is equal, if not superior, to that of their male
counterparts. Women deserve the full respect of men no
matter what the situation.

A woman should enjoy the freedom to excel in virtually
any position, provided she has the appropriate attributes
and qualifications. The aspect of qualification is vital. In the
hiring of an employee the consideration should be, Of all
the applicants, is this the individual best suited to the position? rather than, How many more women do we need to
meet our quota?

Economist Thomas Sowell, renowned black scholar at
the Hoover Institution, has persuasively argued that affirmative action policies, far from benefiting the "minority"
groups they were designed to aid, ultimately backfire
because they generate "artificial [unnecessary, avoidable]
failure." The end result is the reinforcement of myths of
inferiority of the minority group.[13]

Affirmative action policies have been shown to be ineffec-
tive because members of the favored group may slacken
their efforts if they develop a sense of entitlement. While

Sowell's observations were made with regard to racially based policies, they apply directly to the proposed affirmative action policies for women as well.

The concept behind affirmative action hiring is distasteful. Who wouldn't be personally demoralized if he or she were hired instead of a more qualified applicant just because a quota required it? It would be like discovering that the reason a man proposed to you was that he liked your car. Not very flattering! In addition, the practice is unfair to applicants who are better suited for the job.

Finally, a free-market society such as ours cannot be true to its economic principles and at the same time dictate that businesses must make a priority of staffing for social equality. In a struggling economy, common sense requires businesses to hire the best individual for the job. The alternative is nothing short of absurd.

To hire people on the basis of race or gender is no better than refusing to hire on those bases. Just as affirmative action policies at universities have generated artificial academic failure among minority students, such policies for women in the work world would set women up for professional failure. Affirmative action is a misnomer. Far from affirming, it discredits. If a woman is the best candidate for a job, she should be hired for it. If she is not, she should look for a job more suited to her abilities.

We must avoid the "woe is me" syndrome—the fear that we are not getting all we deserve because people aren't treating us fairly. Many of us would do well to follow the example of the chief financial officer at a fast-growing manufacturer of golf clubs. Her perspective on discrimination against women is refreshing and healthy: "Worrying about discrimination is a waste of precious time and energy. I'd rather devote my energy to doing an outstanding job. That's what's going to get you promoted."[14]

THE MYTHICAL GLASS CEILING

You're probably heard about the "glass ceiling"—the obstacle that supposedly keeps women from advancing all the way to the top of a company. In *Fortune* magazine, Nancy Perry talks about why women haven't risen as high as they'd like to go: "One reason more women—and plenty of men—aren't sitting above the glass ceiling is that they haven't tried hard enough to get there."[15]

Is the "glass ceiling" really there, or is it just a figment of someone's imagination? While I think there is some validity to the concept of the glass ceiling, I do not think that men are deliberately working to prevent women from bridging the "great corporate divide." This conspiracy theory is just a bad case of feminist paranoia.

Certainly an "old boy" network exists, and women have learned to form "old girl" networks to assist their juniors. I see nothing wrong with taking a pragmatic approach to assisting one's associates, but to make a doctrine and cause out of the glass ceiling is, I believe, a misuse of time and energy that could better be focused on doing one's job.

> If a woman wants to get ahead in corporate America, she has to put in the same time and energy as a male. . . .
>
> Ardent feminists don't buy this. They dismiss as baloney any factor besides discrimination that might explain why more women aren't running the show. Don't tell them, for example, that part of the reason may be that a sizable share of talented female executives decide to have children and opt out of the chase. . . .
>
> Ironically, many of the same women who fought for choices in the 1960s are the ones now saying it's unfair that women have to make trade-offs between family and career.[16]

In this, as in numerous other issues, feminists act hypo-critically by maintaining a double standard. While protest-ing any discrimination against women, they themselves discriminate against women who disagree with their agenda. When feminists loudly proclaim that more women should be elected to government positions, what they really mean is that more "politically correct" women should fill those vacancies! Only the liberal element of female candi-dates receives support from feminist organizations. Femi-nists have learned that the only way to achieve their liberal goals is to elect like-minded women. Do feminists work to promote women? No, not unless these women espouse femi-nist ideology. So much for shattering the glass ceiling for the good of all!

HEALTH CARE: A WORKING WOMAN'S ISSUE

Some say that health care has become a principal con-cern for baby-boom families and corporations. The cost of medical care for a family with children has escalated to such a degree that unless there is help from the employer's health-care programs, the family begins to suffer. Many cor-porations are staggering under the increased burden of ris-ing health-benefit costs for their employees. The increased costs eventually are passed on to consumers. This increases the cost of living, which in turn increases the necessity for two incomes in the family. Given this scenario, is a national health-care program orchestrated by the government the answer to our health-care woes?

It all boils down to the question of what we expect of gov-ernment. It is very possible that women, who more and more are feeling abandoned by the men in their lives, see their employers much the way they see government—as a dependable authority that provides for and protects them. Wouldn't this explain the emphasis accorded to health care by women? Women feel threatened and alone and therefore sense a need for reliable security—a support for the added burden they must shoulder by themselves.

Government-regulated and -provided health care would probably be a final step in the socialization of our nation. When government begins to regulate what doctors we will see, we have lost a freedom that will never again be regained. In Britain, Canada, and New Zealand, people can wait weeks to see a doctor under their socialized medical programs. The U.S. General Accounting office reported to Congress that Canada's health-care system has major deficiencies. For example, waiting lists for diagnostic procedures and elective surgery may be several months long. It was reported that for cardiovascular surgery urgent patients waited up to one month while elective patients frequently waited up to six months for their surgery.

Government-mandated health care is not concerned with women's best interests. The health-care situation in America does need reform and adjustments, but to hand it entirely over to the government only shifts the problems to a massive structure that has more than enough of its own difficulties. Furthermore, many of the problems in health care have sprung from government intervention. And despite all the talk of controlling the costs, John C. Goodman, president of the National Center for Policy Analysis, has estimated that a Canadian-style system in the United States would cost taxpayers $339 billion in new taxes.

Women need to know the issues, learn from history, and then choose. It is essential that we bear in mind that all of life has consequences. Government-guaranteed health care sounds very appealing at the outset—it promises security, health, and prosperity to all—but it neglects to tell us of the toll it will ultimately take on those it is intended to benefit. Nor does it remind us of the poor quality of service it is destined to deliver.

WOMEN IN COMBAT: WORK WE DON'T NEED

Do women desire to face combat? Apparently a few do. Representative Patricia Schroeder of Colorado has been a leading advocate for this cause, but of course she would never be placed in that position herself.

Sending women to combat may sound absurd. It is worse than that—it is dangerous. Women in the military are not required to perform at the same level as men in physical tests. The standard is greatly lowered in order to accommodate women, who on the average weigh twenty-nine pounds less than men and have twenty-four pounds less muscle than men. Only the top 5 percent of women can be expected to perform at a level equal to that of the average man.

Although physical strength is not a requirement for all occupations in the military, it certainly is vital for combat situations. Let's look at the example of U.S. Army Reserve Staff Sergeant Joni Carter, who, after falling with a sixty-pound rucksack during a combat training exercise, found herself unable to get up. Afterward she noted that during a war that situation would have posed a great danger to her fellow soldiers, with the potential of endangering an entire platoon. Incidentally, Sergeant Carter placed second in her class in her physical fitness test. We see that even the strongest of women could be hazardous to men in combat.

EMPLOYMENT: THE FEMINIST
PROVING GROUND

We cannot hand over the realm of professional employment to the feminists and allow them to pose as women's advocates in a male-dominated world. It would be a pity to suffer as a result of our indifference in yet another feminist-controlled territory of life. Most women do not buy into feminist theory about work.

I was intrigued to find that the *Notre Dame Journal of Law,*

Ethics & Public Policy dedicated an entire issue to the question of women and law. The tone of the articles was set by the foreword, written by law professor Teresa Godwin Phelps. Let me give you a sampling: "If women were to succeed and be equal to men in the workplace," writes Phelps, "other harms had to be abolished; all gender-based exclusions, even if they appeared in the guise of 'job necessities,' had to be eliminated; affirmative action programs that actively encouraged and facilitated women's entry into male dominated fields had to be established."[17]

As I read those lines charting the feminist course, I cannot help thinking of military strategists plotting their way into enemy territory with stealth. Neither I nor the majority of American women share the passion to overpower men that consumes the hard-line feminists. To me, such a cause is a senseless evasion of the real issues of life.

As we have already pointed out, radical feminists would like to eradicate all differences that exist between women and men, including those that are biological. If they could, feminists would remake woman in order to equalize her with her archrival, man. Such an attempt would be futile and could not possibly bring the sense of fulfillment for which feminists long. Power and equality have never brought anyone happiness, but unfortunately, feminists have been blinded to this fact by their own ambition.

What is the prime motivation of feminists who masquerade as compassionate equalizers in the work place? What are the consequences of feminist theories? Dee Jepsen makes the following observations:

> Some women who are pursuing careers, striking out to seek their identity in their credentials and angry at what they view as past "male exploitation," have imitated the characteristics of men. The determined tough-faced women who pursue what has been labeled

a "macho-feminist" course appear to be buying into the male culture they found so offensive in men and are setting aside their womanhood. Ironically, as they struggle to define themselves, they are mimicking the men they resent.[18]

GOD-DIRECTED WORK

God has a plan for each of us, even a work plan. It is good to ask ourselves if we are doing the work God has for us to do. If you are not sure, this should be a focus of prayer for you because God wants his people to be engaged in valuable, rewarding work. We need to seek God's leading in all the work we do, both secular and spiritual, professional and volunteer.

How often do you and I consider volunteer work? Jesus promised to bless the work we do to help others: "And if anyone gives even a cup of cold water to one of these little ones because he is my disciple, I tell you the truth, he will certainly not lose his reward" (Matthew 10:42).

We can learn a lot from that verse. It shows us that it is not so much the nature of the work that gives it meaning, as it is the motive behind our actions. Remember, even if you give all that you own to feed the poor and do any number of other heroic actions, if you are not prompted by love, it will profit you nothing (1 Corinthians 13:3).

Paul approached this subject in his letter to the Corinthian church:

> For we are God's fellow workers; you are God's field, God's building. By the grace God has given me, I laid a foundation as an expert builder, and someone else is building on it. But each one should be careful how he builds. For no one can lay any foundation other than the one already laid, which is Jesus Christ. If any man builds on this foundation using gold, silver, costly

stones, wood, hay or straw, his work will be shown for what it is, because the Day will bring it to light. It will be revealed with fire, and the fire will test the quality of each man's work. If what he has built survives, he will receive his reward. If it is burned up, he will suffer loss; he himself will be saved, but only as one escaping through the flames. (1 Corinthians 3:9-15)

God desires that the work we do bring us enduring joy and satisfaction. This will naturally happen when our efforts are labors of love that bring him glory and praise. After all, it is God who began a good work in us in saving us (Philippians 1:6), and as it says in Ephesians 2:10, we are God's workmanship, his masterpiece, which he is perfecting through Christ so that we might do good works which God prepared beforehand. Our work is really God's work. He deserves the glory for it because it is he who has inspired and equipped us for it. As Isaiah wrote: "LORD . . . all that we have accomplished you have done for us" (Isaiah 26:12).

In light of this, how are we to work? We are to work in the name of the Lord and be thankful for the work opportunities he sends our way. If you are unable to thank the Lord for your work, perhaps you have missed what God really has for you. Examine your heart again and ask God to show you the work he wants you to perform so you can please him. "The steps of a good man [or woman] are ordered by the Lord, and He delights in his way" (Psalm 37:23 NKJV).

If God orders our steps, we can find joy and satisfaction in our work, wherever we do it.

QUESTIONS
FOR REFLECTION AND DISCUSSION

1. How does God view work?
2. What is one of the most noble—if not the most noble—of the professions a woman can have?
3. How challenging is the work of a homemaker?
4. When given the option, should a mother choose to work outside the home?
5. Do affirmative action policies really benefit women?
6. Is it really possible to be Superwoman?
7. How have feminists transformed employment into a proving ground for their objectives?
8. What relationship is there between work and fulfillment?

9

We Want Truth from the "Women's Movement"

If you think equality is the goal . . . your standards are too low.
Women's movement slogan, 1970

Christian women recognize that women deserve equal pay for equal work in the marketplace. We acknowledge that as individuals, women are neither inferior nor superior to men. We cringe and object when women are battered, abused, or degraded. But we must draw the line when the feminists demand that we deny our femininity and our uniqueness. We cannot and must not accept their overblown claims about what a woman should be. Today's feminists are not honest about their beliefs or claims.

In her book *The Power of the Positive Woman,* Phyllis Schlafly includes two pages of pictures the press wouldn't print. The photos were taken at a NOW rally, and they show the lesbians, the socialist organizations, and even the government employees who are behind the feminist movement. Too often we only see the movie stars and celebrities who promote feminism, the pretty people who look good in a ten-second sound bite. But feminism doesn't look so good when we examine it carefully.

As Christian women, we must understand the full implications of the feminist agenda. While feminism has centered attention on some very real societal deficiencies, we must beware of blindly swallowing the story and solution provided by feminism. We must examine the issues in the light of God's Truth.

WHAT FEMINISM SAYS VS. WHAT FEMINISM BELIEVES

Feminism says, "Women are equal to men."
Feminism believes women are better than men.

"The people I'm furious with are the women's liberationists," jokes one writer. "They keep getting up on soapboxes and proclaiming women are brighter than men. That's true, but it should be kept quiet or it ruins the whole racket."[1]

We all like to think we're bright and have ingenious ideas. As women we often perceive things that men never notice—some call this "women's intuition." We like to focus on our excellent qualities, but we are imperfect, flawed beings, just as men are. And if men should not have the final word when it comes to deciding what is true and just, then how can we argue that women should? We need honest solutions to our problems, not hype-driven tirades against men and male organization.

Feminism says, "We want equal opportunity."
Feminism wants to restructure the world.

Feminism today is *not* primarily concerned with issues like equal pay for equal work and protection against sexual harassment. Christina Hoff Sommers describes feminism as a call for a "more radical intellectual, moral, social, and political revolution than the founders of modern Western cultures could have imagined. . . . We are developing a whole reconstruction of the world from the perspective of women with the key word being 'women-centeredness.'"[2]

A leaflet from the Women's International Terrorist Conspiracy from Hell (WITCH) encourages women to join together to overthrow male-dominated society:

> WITCH lives and laughs in every woman. She is the free part of each of us, beneath the shy smiles, the acquiescence to absurd male determination, the make-up or fresh-suffocating clothes our sick society demands. There is no "joining" WITCH. If you are a woman and dare to look within yourself, you are a WITCH. You make your own rules.[3]

What does feminism advocate? Women ruling the world. Female chauvinists claim that if women ruled the world, the great majority of our problems would vanish. Best-selling feminist author Alice Walker feels that the best leadership for the United States would be three grandmothers.

Rebellion is rooted in the call of the women's revolution. You wouldn't be surprised to find Scripture references in this book, but I was astonished to see a Bible verse in Gloria Steinem's book *Outrageous Acts and Everyday Rebellions*. The verse, placed on its own page before the table of contents, was this: "For rebellion is as the sin of witchcraft" (1 Samuel 15:23, KJV). Steinem, who advocates feminist rebellion, quotes the Scripture only to thumb her nose at it.

Rebellion is the core of feminism. Feminism is rebellion against man, against woman, and most tragically, against the God who created us female.

Feminism says, "Women should not have to serve men."
Feminism wants to do without men.

Feminism promotes lesbianism as an alternative to men. We've all heard the popular feminist wisecrack, "A woman

without a man is like a fish without a bicycle," but the Bible
tells us that men and women are mutually dependent
(1 Corinthians 11:11).

Feminism would usurp the role of men. When choosing
a career, the feminist wants to have a traditionally male
job—be it in construction or Congress. Feminists despise
careers traditionally held by women. Feminists bemoan the
fact that "surveys are showing that women's already vast rep-
resentation in the *lowliest occupations* [emphasis added] is
rising."[4]

Feminists not only reject God's design in creation, they
also reject God's plan for the "different yet equal" framework in male/female relationships. They cannot accept
the idea of men and women complementing and complet-
ing each other. Feminists do not acknowledge that there
are true differences—biological, emotional, and social—
between men and women. They will settle for nothing
short of complete role-interchangeability. The ideas that a
man should protect and provide for a woman, and that
a woman should affirm and respond to a man, are considered by feminists to be oppressive goals of Western
patriarchy.

One lesbian proudly proclaimed that she was artificially
inseminated because she wanted to have a child apart from
a man (apparently it never occurred to her that it took a
man to produce the sperm—and ultimately, to produce
her). But after conceiving, she learned the child was a boy,
so she had an abortion. The last thing she wanted to do was
give birth to another "oppressive" male.

"The pitfall of the feminist is the belief that the interests
of men and women can ever be severed; that what brings
suffering to the one can leave the other unscathed," Agnes
Repplier wrote in her book *Points of Friction*.[5] How right she
was—men and women, by God's plan, need each other.

Feminism says, "Women deserve choice."
Feminism wants abortion on demand.

Feminism demands abortion. Since birth control is not always used or does not always work, and since feminists demand the "right" to go to bed with whomever they choose, whenever they want, they feel they *must* have abortion to prevent the unwanted side effects of their behavior—children.

If feminists are really pro-choice and not pro-abortion, why do they scream and organize protests when states pass legislation requiring parental notification or twenty-four hour waiting periods before the unborn child is killed? The reason for notification and waiting periods is to show women they have a choice—a choice for life.

"As long as birth, metaphorically or literally, remains an experience of passively handing over our minds and our bodies to male authority and technology, other kinds of social change can only minimally change our relationship to ourselves, to power, and to the world outside our body," says Adrienne Rich.[6]

Through abortion, feminists have found an avenue for denying the reproductive aspect of their femininity. As one feminist put it, "In a subliminal way, it's revenge against men."[7] No doubt abortion is also rebellion against the Creator—an effort to sabotage his creation. This act of revenge is very often self-directed and ultimately self-destructive.

The Bible speaks clearly on the subject of abortion. God hates the shedding of innocent blood (Proverbs 6:17), and he tells us to deliver those who are being taken away to death and are staggering to slaughter (Proverbs 24:11).

Feminism says, "Women need help with child care."
Feminism wants women to give up child rearing.

Feminism is demanding universal day care as a means of social parenting. "No woman should be authorized to stay at home and raise her children," said the late French feminist Simone de Beauvoir. "Women should not have the choice, precisely because if there is such a choice, too many women will make that one."[8] As a good socialist, Simone de Beauvoir believed that children are the property of the state, and it is therefore the government's duty to take care of them.

Feminism holds that women must be liberated from home and children if they are to be truly human and free. To achieve this goal, the liberated woman is working to restructure our family arrangements. Feminism would grant women access to twenty-four hour child-care services and special privileges at work.

This reluctant attitude toward child rearing has led feminists to reject their own bodies. "Woman has ovaries, a uterus; these peculiarities imprison her in her subjectivity," Simone de Beauvoir said.[9] And according to Margaret Sanger, "No woman can call herself free who does not own and control her body. No woman can call herself free until she can choose consciously whether she will or will not be a mother."[10]

Alison Jaggar, Women's Studies Chair at the University of Cincinnati, eagerly anticipates the day when "the miracle of science will allow us to alter basic human functions like insemination, lactation and gestation. . . . One woman could inseminate another. . . . Men and nonparturitive women could lactate. . . . Fertilized ova could be transferred into women's or even men's bodies."[11]

Feminism implies that women should even reject feminine dress. According to Gloria Steinem, "Even dressing and behaving in a 'feminine' way create a barrier with the natural world, for nature and artifice don't mix well."[12]

WHERE FEMINISTS ARE WRONG

As George Gilder observed in *Men and Marriage,* the so-called women's movement hasn't liberated women at all.

Instead it has freed men from the constraints of traditional morality. As one single woman observed, "When their whole lives men were free to have sex with whomever they wanted, why would they suddenly change after marriage and just have sex with one woman?"

Take a look at a key strategist in the feminist movement, NOW's president, Patricia Ireland. Ireland has learned to become all things to all people in order to accomplish her goals. "It's not smart to make people uncomfortable for reasons apart from the issues," Ireland says.[13] You can be sure that under her direction, the National Organization for Women is not going to publish its full agenda for mass-market consumption—too many people might get the *right* idea and realize the full scope of feminist philosophy.

When confronted with her open lesbianism and adultery—which some in the feminist movement feared would reinforce the public's accurate association of lesbianism with feminism—Ireland explained: "You have to understand that other people's comfort is no longer my job. I am no longer a flight attendant." No, the current president of NOW is also a former corporate lawyer. From the perspective of human relationships, she has married, divorced, remarried, and formed an adulterous relationship with a lesbian. Professionally and philosophically she seems "qualified" to be president of NOW, which represents the radically rebellious women in our nation.

These rebellious women often display arrogance and condescension toward women of unequal educational or professional backgrounds. In this way feminism breeds discontent and unrest: It tells women they need to strive for money, power, and position, as if these are prerequisites for happiness. Educational and professional achievements, they say, are a greater sign of success than motherhood or homemaking.

Like a virus that enters and multiplies in its host's body, feminism has entered into the minds and hearts of many in our nation, distorting normal functions for its own objectives. George Gilder states that the media and politicians are in submission to feminism because the "religions" of the politically correct intellectual class in America are feminism and sexual liberation. Sobering, but true.

GUARD AGAINST INFECTION

As Christians, we are to listen to God rather than the world. It is futile to measure the stature and meaning of your life by comparing it to your neighbor's. Your life is between you and God. Let God set your agenda. Get your cues from God, not from the feminist "experts." After all, he is the one to whom we will each give an account in the end.

In her book *The Feminist Gospel* Mary A. Kassian observes:

> Many Christians view feminism as an ideology that merely promotes the genuine dignity and worth of women. If this were true, feminism would definitely be compatible with Christianity, for the Bible does teach that women and men are of equal value in God's sight, co-created as bearers of God's image. But the philosophy of feminism adds a subtle, almost indiscernible twist to the basic Biblical truth of woman's worth. Feminism asserts that a woman's worth is of such a nature that it gives her the right to discern, judge and govern that truth herself. It infuses women with the idea that God's teaching about the role of women *must* line up with their own perception and definition of equality and/or liberation. Feminism does not present itself as an outright affront to the Bible, but it nevertheless contains an insidious distortion that erodes the authority of Scripture.[14]

The late Christian philosopher Francis Schaeffer said, "Tell me what the world is saying today, and I'll tell you what the church will be saying seven years from now."[15]

Because we live in the world and are affected by it, we need to be on both the offensive and the defensive with regard to the ideas we allow to dwell in our minds. "Principles which one generation accepts provisionally, in the context of other cultural commitments, soon harden into icy dogmas for a generation brought up on nothing else," says journalist Michael Novak.[16]

What worldly principles are we accepting? Those in the women's movement proclaim liberation from men, children, and God, encouraging women to find themselves on their own. In stark contrast, the Bible teaches us to lose our lives, live for others, and pursue the things that will bring glory to God. The two models of living could not be more different.

Feminist philosophy is dangerous not merely because their suggestions ultimately would cause harm to women, but because the motivation behind the movement is clearly rebellion. In their desire to be equal or superior to men, feminists reject God's plan for male leadership in the home and in the church. This rejection is regrettable in the secular world and even more unthinkable in the Christian church, where it has begun to take root.

As women, and as Christians, we are called to be the moral and ethical standard setters as the "salt" and "light" of the world (Matthew 5:13-16). As God's people, we are to be those who season life with righteousness and who expose darkness for what it is. Proverbs 25:26 warns us that "like a muddied spring or a polluted well is a righteous man who gives way to the wicked." We must be prepared to stand against the tide and resist the spread of infectious ideologies. We must guard against deception, and our own lives should exemplify the standards God sets before us. We must live for truth and not merely profess it.

The next time you shop for groceries, look at the typical selection of women's magazines in your grocery store.

Emblazoned boldly on their covers are articles promoting women's self-esteem, self-help, and self-worth. One magazine challenges you to find sexual satisfaction without a man; another accuses your husband of having an extramarital affair. The subtle voice of deceit whispers that perhaps you should experience something new just to experiment and add a little excitement in your life. The voices are whispering—are you listening?

Until Christ's return, life on earth will be a continuous series of spiritual battles. Satan, the enemy of our souls, is not asleep. He knows his time is short, and he is determined to make the most of his opportunities. Are you aware of the attacks waged against you? Do they catch you off guard? We must learn to be vigilant soldiers, armed with the weapons of God described in the sixth chapter of Ephesians: the full armor of God, the belt of truth, the breastplate of righteousness, feet fitted with the readiness that comes from the gospel of peace, the shield of faith, the helmet of salvation, and the sword of the Spirit, the Word of God.

After Moses' death, the Lord exhorted Joshua to keep his word in his heart: "Do not let this Book of the Law depart from your mouth; meditate on it day and night, so that you may be careful to do everything written in it. Then you will be prosperous and successful" (Joshua 1:8).

What a priceless promise! If we spend time meditating on God's Word and determine to obey it fully, we are assured success in all we do. Why are we so slow to follow God's formula? Perhaps it is because we are hearing—and heeding—the words of the world. Let us remember our Lord's teaching: "No one can serve two masters. Either he will hate the one and love the other, or he will be devoted to the one and despise the other" (Matthew 6:24). Indeed, women cannot serve God and feminism.

HOW LIES GAIN ACCEPTANCE

Herbert Agar once said, "The truth that makes men free is for the most part the truth which men prefer not to hear." As Christian women, we want God's truth to be reflected in society. Not man's truth, or the recently upgraded and improved "truth" we hear each morning as the latest news flash on the morning talk shows, but the eternal, lasting truth of God's Word.

Satan's lies have a way of subtly becoming accepted as truth. There's an old axiom—if you tell a lie long enough, sooner or later people believe it. Elbert Hubbard described the process in which a lie becomes man's truth this way:

> Truth, in its struggles for recognition, passes through four distinct stages. First, we say it is damnable, dangerous, disorderly, and will surely disrupt society. Second, we declare it is heretical, infidelic, and contrary to the Bible. Third, we say it is really a matter of no importance either one way or the other. Fourth, we aver that we have always upheld and believed it.[17]

Take, for instance, the commonly accepted belief that homosexuality is a morally neutral inborn quality, like skin color or height. No one would have dreamed of allowing special laws for those who practice sexual perversion fifty years ago. No one would have predicted that some feminists would praise lesbianism as a way to live happily without men.

But look how times have changed. Now we think it a great virtue to be "accepting." The nation's advice columnists proclaim that homosexuality is just another way of life. Schools teach children that daddies may live and sleep with other daddies. And those who consider themselves enlightened accept this "truth" and pride themselves on their tolerance.

What has happened to truth? Surely we deserve to see it

reflected in our society! Frank Norris, writing in *The Respon-sibilities of the Novelist,* agrees:

> The people have a right to the Truth as they have a right to life, liberty and the pursuit of happiness. It is *not* right that they be exploited and deceived with false views of life, false characters, false sentiment, false morality, false history, false philosophy, false emotions, false heroism, false notions of self-sacrifice, false views of religion, of duty, of conduct and manners.[18]

Today we have strayed far from God's truth and his original intention for us. He planned for men and women to marry and share a lifetime commitment to each other. The sexual relationship that God provided was meant for marriage only. Sex was designed for men and women; sex between same-sex partners is condemned by God. But today the prevailing worldly wisdom, accepted even by many Christians, holds that biology determines sexual orientation and behavior, and anyone who dares argue against such claims is usually labeled "homophobic" or a "gay basher."

Satan's lies about abortion are also commonly accepted. We are told the unborn child is not a baby, but simply a "fetus" or a "product of conception," and therefore abortion is seen as an inoffensive, harmless procedure. We are told that "quality of life" is more important than life itself, and therefore infanticide and euthanasia lurk around the door of every hospital.

THE BIGGEST LIE

Why does our society so readily substitute lies for God's eternal truth? Because over the last hundred years, we have come to accept one of Satan's biggest lies: evolution. This has in turn prepared the way for all the lies that have followed. By substituting a lie for truth to answer the simple question, Where did we come from? Satan has destroyed our foundation for godly living.

God's truth is that we came from God's hand. As his creation, we are valuable. If we believe this, we know that we have inestimable worth, and that we also have a responsibility to live as our Creator planned.

By contrast, if we sprang from algae growing on a space rock, we are of no more eternal significance than a dead tree stump in a forgotten field, which no doubt can trace its origins to similar algae. With no eternal value, why should we think that our actions are important?

But the truth that we are God's creation has been forcibly removed from our public schools. Teachers tell our children that the earth is millions of years old and that life evolved from nothing. Despite the fact that evolution is simply a theory, and that scientists disagree among themselves as to how it may have happened, still our schools prefer to teach that life came about by accident rather than from the hand of God himself.

It is to our society's shame that an alternate belief, such as special creation by God, cannot legally even be discussed in a public school classroom. God has been removed from our public schools, and the door has been left wide open for man's "wisdom" instead of God's truth.

What has rushed through the open door to fill the vacuum? Acceptance of all kinds of behaviors and practices contrary to our Creator's plan: feminism, abortion, gay and lesbian "families," promiscuity, sexual perversions.

By doubting God's truth about creation, we have set ourselves up for a tidal wave of doubt that will destroy our very foundations. In 2 Peter 2 we learn that if we forget truth and walk according to our own wisdom, with lust, rebellion, and self-will, we will receive punishment at the Day of Judgment. In chapter 3 Peter warns us that "in the last days scoff-

ers will come, scoffing and following their own evil desires"
(2 Peter 3:3).

Who are today's scoffers? Evolutionists who deny God as
Creator. Feminists who reject the roles of men and women
that God established. Abortionists who refuse to acknowledge unborn babies as children. Homosexuals who deny
that their behavior is sin. Sex educators who teach children
how to make promiscuity less dangerous but who say nothing about moral standards.

God does not forget what he has promised to those who
willfully reject his commands. But God promises peace to
those who do not swallow the lies that Satan has planted in
our society. In the midst of opposition, conflict, and a topsy-
turvy world, we will be found without spot and blameless
(2 Peter 3:14).

"Man has no nobler function than to defend the truth,"
Ruth McKenney wrote.[19] As women of God, we want the
women's movement to be truthful with us about their aims.
We want society to make truth a foundational part of public
policy. We do not want America to fall under God's judg-
ments because we have chosen lies instead of truth.

We know that God's truth is found only in God's Word.
We must defend that truth in our homes, in our schools,
and in our country.

QUESTIONS
FOR REFLECTION AND DISCUSSION

1. What is the central principle of the feminist movement?
2. In what ways is feminism incompatible with Christianity?
3. Is it biblically consistent to be a "Christian feminist"?
4. How has rejecting God's truth affected our society?
5. What can women do to defend God's truth in our homes, our schools, and our nation?
6. What worldly principles have we accepted into our thinking?
7. Is "quality of life" ever as important as life itself?
8. In what ways is the feminist argument for "reproductive choice" based on a fallacy?
9. What do feminists really want?
10. Why are the feminists fighting a losing battle?

10

We Want to Find Our Rightful Place in the Church

"The Church cannot be restricted to the sanctuary," Francis J. Lally once told interviewer Mike Wallace. "The Church isn't just a preaching Church, a sacramental Church, but is involved in the total life of the human being, which is another way of saying religion has implications in society."[1]

Religion—and church—do have a role in society, and as women, we should have a role in the church. But what should we want—and expect—our role to be? Before we delve into a woman's specific place in the church, we need to understand God's plan for the church in the world.

THE GLORIOUS CHURCH OF JESUS CHRIST

As Christians, we are distinctly blessed to be part of the church—Christ's body, "the fullness of him who fills every-thing in every way" (Ephesians 1:23) and "the pillar and foundation of the truth" (1 Timothy 3:15). While Christ is preparing a place for us in heaven, he has given us the task of being his arms, his heart, his voice, his *body*, in a sorrowful and needy world.

Practically, the church is the coming together of God's people who meet for communion with God and fellowship with one another. We need each other in order to function individually. We have individual gifts, described in 1 Corinthians 12, and we work together in sync to bring glory to God. None of the members of the body is to be rejected or belittled. We are all to depend on each other. In a properly functioning church, when believers gather together, their individual gifts inspire and equip each other for ministry.

A healthy church "spreads everywhere the fragrance of the knowledge of him. For we are to God the aroma of Christ among those who are being saved and those who are perishing" (2 Corinthians 2:14-15). When the church is in all her splendor—"without stain or wrinkle or any other blemish" (Ephesians 5:27)—she is a marvelous sight to behold! It is then that the church is truly the salt of the earth and the light of the world.

The church is made up of individuals, and she will only be as "holy and without blemish" as the members are. It behooves us all, men and women, to forget ourselves and glorify the Lord so the church can be everything that Christ intended her to be.

Jesus said that he would build his church and that the gates of hell would not prevail against it (Matthew 16:18, KJV). It is good to remember those words, especially when it looks as though the gates of hell are winning! The church of Jesus Christ has always been in enemy territory and will continue to be until Christ returns to do away with every one of the devil's destructive designs. And though the world continues to grow dark, we can rejoice in our opportunity to *shine!* "The path of the righteous is like the first gleam of dawn, shining ever brighter till the full light of day" (Proverbs 4:18).

Not only do we have the opportunity to shine, we have a unique challenge. Ephesians 3:10 tells us that God's intention is "that now, through the church, the manifold wisdom of God should be made known to the rulers and authorities in the heavenly realms." God is using us to fight in the spiritual warfare in these last days. We are his body, and he is our head.

For these reasons, it is essential that we stay attached to our head, Christ, and allow him to direct us. As it so often says in the book of Revelation, "He who has an ear, let him hear what the Spirit says to the churches."

A FOUNDATION AND A REFUGE

Earlier I referred to the verse in 1 Timothy 3 that tells us the church is the "pillar and foundation of the truth." As the pillar, the church is to stand firm against the weight of opposition. As the foundation, the church is the basis of truth.

There has been much talk of the cultural and ethical crisis facing our nation and the need to return to traditional values, but people fail to associate a high standard of ethics with its true source: the knowledge of God. Our modern culture is blind! In order to maintain high moral values, all societies must know and revere God. It is impossible for America to ever win the battle for integrity unless we return to the Judeo-Christian ethic upon which we were founded. Our country has forfeited the firm footing from which it could attack lawlessness. As Charles Colson so succinctly put it:

> In an age that celebrates tolerance as its supreme virtue, no absolute standard of right and wrong—which by definition excludes other standards—can be adopted. Nor can any satisfactory code of ethics.
>
> If a consensus in our society really wants ethics on Capitol Hill, on Wall Street, in the worlds of business and academia, we must be willing to base those ethics on a *firm foundation*. And in Western civilization that foundation has been twenty-three centuries of accumu-

lated wisdom, natural law, and the Judeo-Christian tradition based on Biblical revelation.[2]

The world's problem—its lack of a firm foundation—becomes the church's problem when the church shoots itself in the foot by refuting the inerrancy of Scripture. When the church upholds the truth, light will shine, people will see, and righteousness will be lifted up. Remember, the devil is as crafty and subtle with his "logic" today as he was in the Garden all those years ago.

Armed with the Word of God, the church can provide women with a foundation for living and be a refuge in time of trouble. Wherever a woman may find herself in life—young, old, single, married, with or without children, family, friends, a job—the church can meet her needs.

In a world where the hearts of men and women are growing colder by the minute (Matthew 24:12), a woman can find an oasis in her church home. There she can receive Christ's love, compassion, concern, and provision, because as Christ is, so is the church in the world. "Love is made complete among us so that we will have confidence on the day of judgment, because in this world we are like him" (1 John 4:17).

SALT, LIGHT, AND LOVE

The church and its members are to be like salt in the world—seasoning, preserving, and healing. We are to define with seasoning an otherwise tasteless reality, preserve the truth, and lead those who have been hurt and wronged to healing in Christ. When an outright wrong exists in the world—abortion or homosexuality, for examples—the church must speak out against these sins (Proverbs 24:11-12).

As light, we are to expose the evil in the world. By God's design, this happens naturally when we live pure and blameless lives. Christians may find themselves, like Daniel, scrutinized by an incredulous group of observers. What an excellent testimony we would offer if what was written about Daniel could be written about us as well:

> Now Daniel so distinguished himself among the administrators and the satraps by his exceptional qualities that the king planned to set him over the whole kingdom. At this, the administrators and the satraps tried to find grounds for charges against Daniel in his conduct of government affairs, but they were unable to do so. They could find no corruption in him, because he was trustworthy and neither corrupt nor negligent. (Daniel 6:3-4)

Why do we want to preserve the world with our salt and expose the truth with our light? Because Jesus commanded us to do so, like him, we love the world and long for its salvation.

From the beginning we were told to love—first God, and then our neighbors as ourselves. These are, in fact, the two most critical commandments of the Scriptures (Matthew 22:37-40). If we are not loving, we are missing the blessing of God. As the Bible teaches in 1 Corinthians 13, none of the good deeds we do for others is of any lasting benefit if we do these things for any reason apart from love. But love never fails. We must, therefore, start with love and go where it leads us.

Paul wrote that we are called to freedom in Christ. We are to use this freedom, not for selfish purposes, but as an opportunity to serve others in love (Galatians 5:13). Our Lord Jesus said that the love Christians have for one another would show all men that they are his disciples (John 13:35).

> Dear friends, let us love one another, for love comes
> from God. Everyone who loves has been born of God
> and knows God. Whoever does not love does not know
> God, because God is love. . . . Dear friends, since God
> so loved us, we also ought to love one another. (1 John
> 4:7-8, 11)

Unlike the worldly feminist who lives only for herself, the
Christian woman gives of herself. The two mind-sets could
not be more radically opposed to each other. The feminist
wants to get all she can while giving as little as possible. In
her mind, she has to grab all she can from life because
nobody will give her what she wants. In this respect, feminism is nothing but childishness in a mature-looking pack-
age.

Christianity, on the other hand, calls men and women to
deny themselves, take up their crosses, and follow Christ
wherever he leads us. No card-carrying feminist can go
where Christ goes, for he came to give up his rights and
lose his life.

> Your attitude should be the same as that of Christ
> Jesus: Who, being in very nature God, did not con-
> sider equality with God something to be grasped, but
> made himself nothing, taking the very nature of a ser-
> vant, being made in human likeness. And being found
> in appearance as a man, he humbled himself and
> became obedient to death—even death on a cross!
> (Philippians 2:5-8)

That's the example the Lord set for us. As his children,
we ought to worship him in humility and truth. He has
promised that in being lifted up, he will draw all men to
himself (John 12:32).

MEETING NEEDS: PHYSICAL AND SOCIAL

Christ came to earth to meet our need for salvation, healing, and hope. He gave his life for all who would receive him. In turn, as his body on earth, the church is responsible to be a vessel for compassion, generosity, love, and forgiveness.

Single mothers are among the neediest people in America today. Due to unfortunate circumstances, they have found themselves raising children without the much-needed assistance of a husband and father for their children. This is where the church family must come to the rescue. I know of churches where single mothers are helped by members who baby-sit for them, prepare and deliver meals, pray with them, give financial gifts, drive them to church on Sunday, and assist in many other ways. Many churches have support groups for single moms. This is love in action, and love has a remarkable healing effect on hurting people.

Meeting needs through the church has biblical precedents. In the New Testament we read of the disciples selling their possessions in order to share with the truly needy (Acts 2:44-45). In those days, needs were primarily met by family members rather than government, and if a person did not have family to provide help, the church would gather as a family to provide. As the bride of Christ, the church was providing generosity and nurturing care.

The church can meet more than physical needs, and it can help more than adults. Proverbs 13:20 tells us that "he who walks with the wise grows wise, but a companion of fools suffers harm." As social creatures, you and I are naturally affected by the company we keep. So are our children.

Children are as susceptible to influence—good and bad—today as they have been in previous generations, but evil and corruption abound today as never before in recent history. Even members of the media acknowledge the need for a moral cleanup! Most parents feel helpless to combat the negative influences of television, videos, movies, magazines, and music on young people, especially when they spend less and less time with their children.

That is why parents need to find a solid, Bible-teaching church that has a good youth program. In such a church, children and teens can participate in church athletic activities, Bible studies, camp experiences, and outreach programs. Even more important, they can make Christian friends who will encourage them to take a bold stand for Christ when they are away from the wholesome environment of church.

In an effort to combat the dreadful moral collapse of our society, many churches have established schools in which their children can mature both academically and spiritually. Morally upright children don't "just happen" in our day and age. Today it takes the home, church, and school all working in harmony together to bring our children through the "mine fields" that would destroy them. The church, as the pillar and foundation of truth, is the perfect medium for propagating the truth that will protect and preserve our youth.

Don't let your kids be bored at church. Even if it means changing churches, find a youth program that will interest them and also fill them with godly principles.

FEMINIST PHILOSOPHY IN THE CHURCH

As the church has grown and sought to spread the gospel of Jesus Christ, society has brought pressures upon it. As I travel across the United States and speak with thousands of Christian women, it has become more and more apparent that the church has not been immune to the feminist ideologies blanketing our society. Philosophical battle lines are being drawn even in the church itself. As women seek their role in church ministry, two opposing forces are taking sides: the traditionalists, who believe in the inerrancy of the Scriptures; and the Christian feminists, who would like to see Scripture loosely interpreted to fit their ideas.

Many times this church division occurs gradually as restless women drift away from the absolutes in the Word of God. The differences may at first be minimal, but the gap between the two groups has been widening. This trend is occurring even in traditionally conservative, fundamentalist churches, but it has been more obvious in the mainline denominations.

Letha Scanzoni, Nancy Hardesty, and Virginia Ramey Mollenkott are among the Christian feminists who have made inroads into the church for the promotion of feminism and demotion of the Bible. They challenge not only church hierarchy, but the validity of Scripture itself. This movement spells clear and present danger for the church.

Mary A. Kassian, author of *The Feminist Gospel: The Movement to Unite Feminism with the Church,* says, "Biblical feminists have stepped over the line delineating the Christian worldview from the feminist one by accepting the feminist logic that allows them to place themselves above the Bible in respect to male and female roles."[3] Christian feminists have gone at least one step too far in placing their faulty judgment above the flawless Word of God.

Feminism pushes for the ordination of women in Christian churches. In many instances the feminists have met with success in this area, to the peril of the church. The dean of the National Cathedral, an Episcopal institution in our nation's capital, says that refusing the ordination of women is a "misuse of the faith."[4] The Episcopal church has already ordained female bishops, and the ordination of women opens the door for homosexuals who will use similar arguments of oppression and bigotry to press for their unscriptural aspirations.

Not surprisingly, Gloria Steinem praises the Episcopal church's "progress" in religious matters:

> It gave me a new respect for all those working to reform organized religion from within, whether they were tracing the Black Madonna of Eastern Europe back to the Great Cosmic Mother of Africa or bringing an ecclesiastical lawsuit in support of the ordination of women as Episcopalian priests.[5]

RELIGION BY DEMOCRACY

Why shouldn't a woman be ordained to the pastoral ministry? We must find our answer in God's Word. My desire and purpose is to relate a woman's role to the authority of Scripture—the only absolute truth. God does not contradict his principles. If I stray from biblical teaching, then I have lost my foundation. The conscientious Christian woman will be more concerned with the biblical teachings on this subject than she will with the secular, sociological pressures regarding the "rights" of women.

No doubt feminists Letha Scanzoni and Nancy Hardesty have contributed to this confusion over scriptural teaching through their writings regarding women in the church. They are adamant that women be allowed to fill positions in the church that previously have been limited to men. This is their argument:

> Overall, it is clear that while many people feel they are arguing on the basis of scriptural prohibitions, they are simply standing on theological tradition based on cultural prejudices. What they are saying is that for one sex, half the human race, sexual differentiation is a handicap so crippling that no amount of personal talent, intelligence, piety, or even divine enabling, can make them ministers of the gospel.[6]

If the qualifications for being a minister were personal talents or gifts, there would be no question about whether or not women should be ordained for the ministry. Certainly there are many women who would qualify under those standards. However, these two authors have dismissed what the Scriptures say about women in ministry as "theological tradition based on cultural prejudices." I cannot summarily dismiss any part of the Word of God.

I recently learned of a pastor in Oak Park, Illinois, who took the bold step of instructing his congregation on the issue of biblical manhood and womanhood. Recognizing that both worldly extremes on the issue of women's roles—male chauvinism and radical feminism—are harmful and destructive, this pastor was seeking to impart to his congregation a sound biblical perspective:

> It's not just a cultural or social or political issue. It's also a deeply-felt spiritual and theological question. All across America the mainline denominations are electing women to positions formerly held only by men. Women now serve as deacons, elders, pastors, and bishops. Such a mighty institution as the Roman Catholic Church has been shaken in recent years by a massive protest against an all-male priesthood. Here in Oak Park several mainline churches have female pastors and one Catholic church drew nationwide attention when Sister Teresita was removed from giving the homily during Mass.
>
> But the debate comes even closer to home. The feminist movement has at last entered the evangelical movement—producing something called "evangelical feminism." Certain professors and theologians have won notoriety for their books calling for an end to the practice of male-only elders and pastors. What makes their approach unique is that they argue from within

the evangelical framework of belief in the inspiration of Scripture and the deity of Jesus Christ. In effect, they are evangelicals arguing against the long-held position of male headship—at least as that position has been traditionally understood.[7]

It is refreshing to hear these problems being addressed by sound biblical pastors. But more often than not, we hear of decisions to move away from the Scriptures rather than into conformity with them. A case in point is the Church of England, which voted to allow the ordination of women late in 1992. This decision was reached by vote, not by reference to the unchanging Word of God. It was another case of religion by democracy.

The Anglicans have joined numerous other Christian denominations in which women now serve as deacons, elders, pastors, and bishops. Needless to say, the fact that the Anglicans are in good company numerically does not constitute a biblically solid decision.

Nothing is sacred to feminists, who view the church as just another frontier awaiting their arrival. As in any other domain of life, they have applied the standard doctrine of egalitarianism and role-interchangeability to the question of women's roles in the church.

WOMEN'S SCRIPTURAL ROLE

What is the proper role of women in the church? According to Scriptures, women and men are spiritually equal. Both are commanded to obey God; both are instructed to teach their children; and both are allowed to participate fully in church services and sacraments.

Women have the same access to God as men. The Scriptures tell us of many times when God dealt directly with women. For example, he sent angels to Hagar, the mother of Samson, and Mary. But Scripture further tells us that women did not serve in positions of leadership as apostles, pastors, evangelists, or elders. According to God's design, those positions are to be filled by men.

As John MacArthur explains,

> Women have an important place in the plan of God, and they are equal with men spiritually. However, they are not to function in the same role as men. Because women are spiritually equal, Paul insisted that they be given the same opportunities to learn as men. Women cannot teach spiritual truths to their children, lead people to Christ, or obey God if they are not given the opportunity to learn. Paul wanted to clearly teach that the differences in roles between men and women do not in any way imply the spiritual inferiority of women.[8]

"Biblical feminists" like to quote Galatians 3:28, claiming that it means that there are no distinctions between men and women: "There is neither Jew nor Greek, slave nor free, male nor female, for you are all one in Christ Jesus."

But, clearly, there *are* distinctions. Paul was not writing that distinctions such as those between Jews and Greeks, slaves and free, male and female did not exist in the world. Slaves did exist in Paul's day, and Paul wrote that they were to serve their masters well. If there were no differences between men and women, it would make no difference whether a woman married a man or a woman; but God makes it clear over and over in his Word that homosexuality is an abomination to him. Obviously, differences exist in the world, and we must live with those differences as God has commanded us.

Paul was making the point that men and women are equally sinful and equally redeemable by the sacrificial death of Christ. Missing the point, many feminists continue to argue that men and women are interchangeable. To infer that men and women have the same function in the body of Christ from Galatians 3:28 is taking this Scripture out of context.

We can't deny, however, that there have been real problems in the church with regard to the treatment of women. As Mary Kassian notes in her book *The Feminist Gospel*, too often men have been authoritarian, domineering, and proud, while women have been passive and insecure. Locked into stereotypical roles of service and behavior, men and women have not thrived according to God's plan. This is not the biblical model; the Bible teaches that women in the church must be treated as coheirs of the grace of life (1 Peter 3:7), equal and yet different, distinct from men but equal and just as vital. We must seek to complete, rather than compete with, each other.

As Christians, our goal is not to "find ourselves," but to lose ourselves. Paradoxically, it is in losing ourselves that we find life. Jesus told us, "If anyone would come after me, he must deny himself and take up his cross daily and follow me. For whoever wants to save his life will lose it, but whoever loses his life for me will save it" (Luke 9:23-24).

Christianity is incompatible with seeking full possession of our individual rights. To say we serve Christ while serving only ourselves is antithetical. A life focused on self—me, my, mine—cannot bring happiness. Any woman who emphasizes her personal rights will breed discontent. Men and women alike are called to abdicate their "rights" and lose their lives for the sake of others. This is, after all, the example Jesus Christ left for us.

THE MYSTERY OF HEADSHIP

When a church begins to question the Bible's inerrancy and cultural relevance, it steps onto the slippery slope of moral relativism on which it is nearly impossible to regain firm footing. If people view God's Word as "evolving" in order to conform to the current culture, before long biblical prohibitions (such as the ordination of women, homosexuality, adultery, divorce, euthanasia, and abortion) are perceived as acceptable.

Without the traction provided by God's revealed will to keep us on the right road, people slip and fall. We need to realize that God and his Word are constant. We must return to the pure, unchanging standards of the Bible.

The Bible's directives do not always agree with the "politically correct" opinion. But the answer is not found in what the Presbyterians, Methodists, Catholics, Baptists, or Pentecostals teach; nor is it found in what feminists, Christian or otherwise, advocate. The basis for our understanding the role of women must be what the Word of God says about women in the church.

In Ephesians 5 Paul compared the husband/wife relationship to that of Christ and his bride, the church. The passage teaches us that wives are to be subject to their husbands, just as the church is to be subject to Christ. The church and the wife are interchangeable in this example, as are Christ and the husband. Christ and the husband are heads of the church and the wife respectively (Ephesians 5:23), and Christ is the head of every man (1 Corinthians 11:3). Paul conceded that this is a great mystery (Ephesians 5:32), but it is a "heavenly truth" to be enacted in the church and in the Christian home. Male and female are "one in Christ" (Galatians 3:28), and yet the man is the head of the woman (1 Corinthians 11:3). This is another facet of the great mystery.

> Male headship means that a man has a holy obligation
> before God to lay down his life for his wife, his chil-
> dren, his family, friends, and for the people of his own
> congregation. For a husband, it means that he has his

wife's best interests at heart, that he sacrifices his own desires for hers, that he puts her first always in his affections. For an elder in the local church, it means that he leads first, last and always by serving others. For a woman, submission in this context means believing that God is able to work through your husband to accomplish his will in your life, to protect your interests, and to meet your deepest needs. It also means believing that God can do the same thing through the leaders of your church.[9]

When the truth of male headship is denied, the teaching of Ephesians 5 is destroyed. If we argue that a man should not be the head of a woman, then Christ should not be the head of the church. God forbid!

GODLY WOMEN OF THE PAST

Throughout history, women have had a vital part in the local church—not in the leadership, but always in the ministry of service. Paul apparently admired female church workers and considered them his friends and co-laborers, because he mentions them many times. Romans 16 is Paul's record of special recognition given to numerous servants of Christ, several of whom are women. This passage exemplifies the biblical view of women as coworkers. In it we see that far from belittling women, Paul has a glowing appreciation for women and their service for Christ.

Women were involved in many diverse areas of ministry. A partial list follows:

- *Hospitality*—Lydia (Acts 16:15, 40) opened her home as a base for outreach and discipleship. Nympha (Colossians 4:15) opened her home for church meetings.
- *Service*—Phoebe (Romans 16:1-2) was called a "servant of the church" (today more commonly called a

deacon). Dorcas (Acts 9:36) abounded with deeds of kindness and charity, which she performed continually.

- *Labor*—Mary (Romans 16:6) worked hard for the church. Tryphena and Tryphosa (Romans 16:12) were probably sisters who worked hard for the Lord.
- *Prophecy*—Four daughters of Philip (Acts 21:8-9, NASB) were virgins "who were prophetesses."
- *Teaching*—Priscilla (Acts 18:26; Romans 16:3) taught the way of God with her husband. She was called a fellow worker in Christ Jesus.

Each of these women worked under the leadership and authority of local churches led by men. They were using their gifts, yet they remained in obedience to Jesus Christ. In the church, authority is in the hands of men because they represent Christ. To disagree is to reject Christ's authority as head of the church.

The ultimate goal of the total ministry of the church is to introduce people to Christ and to teach them the Word of God for their spiritual growth. This area of service is open to every Christian, male and female; in fact, we are all commanded to be witnesses of Christ.

If the desire of women who campaign for female ordination is to be able to win others to Christ and teach the Word, this is already commanded. A person does not need ordination papers to bring someone to Christ or to lead a Bible study. However, if the motivation is to attain leadership over a congregation, then it becomes a selfish desire for an elevated position. The Bible gives the man that responsibility in the church, as Christ's representative.

UNPOPULAR SUBMISSION

Just as women are exhorted to submit to their husbands at home, they are also to be under the authority of the ministers of their local churches. This is true whether they are single or married. All Christian women are to be in an attitude of submission, both at home and at church.

This is not a popular teaching, because current culture programs women to demand their "rights." The feminist revolution is even affecting attitudes toward scriptural truths. A reminder of the instructions from 2 Peter may help the Christian woman take her eyes off sociological trends and return to the truth in the Word:

> Therefore, dear friends, since you already know this, be on your guard so that you may not be carried away by the error of lawless men and fall from your secure position. But grow in the grace and knowledge of our Lord and Savior Jesus Christ. (2 Peter 3:17-18)

Our growth is to be in the "grace and knowledge of our Lord . . . Jesus Christ," and not in our personal rights and privileges. We cannot use human reason to justify the place of women in the church, for this truth is heavenly and beyond human understanding. As Paul said, "It is a great mystery." But its application to our lives, no matter how illogical or unfair in the eyes of the world, will result in God's blessing. Therefore we must accept it, trusting the almighty God, who designed us for a definite purpose.

QUESTIONS
FOR REFLECTION AND DISCUSSION

1. What is a biblical view of the church?
2. How do you know a healthy church when you see it?
3. What is the church's rightful role in the world?
4. What is a woman's rightful role in the church?
5. How is the church to be the "pillar and foundation" of truth in the world?
6. Why is it important for Christian women to be actively involved in a local church?
7. In what ways is the church uniquely equipped to meet the needs of women?
8. What can we do to guard against the infiltration of feminism and other false doctrines into our churches?

11

We Want Our Desires Respected by Government

Picture this: you have excavated and dug deeply into the soil until you reach rock. Now you are building a massive structure that you hope will endure several generations. The painstaking work is one of love and faith, for you will not live to see the finished product. Still, as a visionary, you labor tirelessly. Constructing with only the finest, most durable materials, you and your co-laborers struggle in this toil of a lifetime, teaching those of the next generation the methods and means needed to continue the work. They, in turn, take up the hammer at the end of your days. The cycle continues.

After some time, however, the initial vision wears thin and the laborers decide their personal interests and pleasure are more worthy pursuits than the construction of this magnificent structure. In their indifference and indolence, this new generation of laborers begins to build with easier methods and cheaper materials. They begin work later and end earlier each day. They compromise a little here, a little there. The change of heart is evident in the construction. It has begun to resemble the leaning tower of Pisa—a far cry from what the original builders intended.

The purists among the builders find this shift in construction unsatisfactory and voice their alarm. They bring out a copy of the blueprints of the building and show it to the other workers. "Oh, how magnificent our edifice would be if constructed to design!" they exclaim. "But what a supreme waste of effort, potential, and time if we continue to build without vision or heart!"

The parallels between that description and our nation today are evident. A potentially magnificent structure has fallen into the hands of hirelings who have gone against the architects' original intent. Our nation was founded on the wise principles of the Bible, and yet we have abused the glorious foundation. We are constructing instead a matchbox casino designed for immediate gratification and corresponding devastation.

All is not well in America.

WHAT IS GOVERNMENT?

What is government, and what should we expect of it? Government exists on many levels, starting with self-government and ending with civil government.

> The word government meant, *first* of all, the self-government of the Christian man, the basic government in all history. *Second,* and almost inseparably linked with this, government meant the family. Every family is a government; it is man's first church and first school, and also his first state. The government of the family by God's appointed head, the man, is basic to society. *Third,* the church is a government, with laws and discipline. *Fourth,* the school is an important form of government in the life of a child. *Fifth,* business or vocations are an important area of government. Our work clearly governs us and we govern our work. *Sixth,* private associations, friendships, organizations, and

the like act as a government over us, in that we submit to these social standards and we govern others by our social expectations. *Seventh,* the state is a form of government. Originally, it was always called civil government in distinction from all these other forms of government.

But tragically, today when we say *government* we generally mean only the state, the federal government, or some other form of civil government. And, more tragically, civil government today claims to be *the* government over man, not just one government among many. Civil government claims jurisdiction over our private associations, our work or business, our schools and churches, our families, and over ourselves. The word government no longer means self-government primarily and essentially; it means the state.[1]

According to the United States Constitution, our government exists to promote domestic tranquility and provide for the common defense. In order to promote domestic tranquility, it may well be the government's role to provide cultural safeguards for the family and the home, such as laws that prohibit pornography, child molestation, forcible rape, etc.

But while our government still exhibits a few vestiges of its original design, much of its foundation has been destroyed. "The deterioration of a government begins almost always with the decay of its principles," wrote the French philosopher Montesquieu.[2] I firmly believe that our decaying moral principles are leading to the destruction of what we've always valued in the United States of America.

TRUSTING THE WRONG PROVIDER
Americans are caught up in a trend that is leading us deeper and deeper into sin and further and further away from God's Word. Though most Americans do not think

our government is efficient, still many people look to government to cure all our economic and social ills. Where once churches, neighbors, and communities were looked upon to help the needy and maintain their individual communities, the federal government is now seen as the almighty provider.

We have failed to trust God and each other; instead we have developed a habit of looking to government to care for us. Women are especially prone to this attitude, partially because a great many of society's ills involve women. Studies show that most single mothers will sink to poverty at some point in their lives and live on welfare. When faced with the troubling issues of abortion, homelessness, educational reform, and prenatal care, women turn to the government for help.

We forget that the government is an institution created by God to be organized *by* the people and *for* the people. Government was never intended to take on a life and personality of its own, but today our government has its own morals, ethics, and standards by which all its citizens must live. Listen to former president Woodrow Wilson:

> Liberty has never come from the government. Liberty has always come from the subjects of it. The history of liberty is a history of resistance. The history of liberty is a history of limitations of governmental power, not the increase of it.[3]

In a poll conducted for CNN and *Time* magazine in 1989, one thousand adults were asked which level of government responded best to their individual needs. Forty percent said their local government responded best; 21 percent said their state government; and 18 percent said the federal government.[4] The reason for the differences is not hard to figure out. The local government knows who they are because it is made up of people in their community.

We are much more likely to become involved in community matters than in federal matters, primarily because we can see and feel the effects individually. In 1992 members of Concerned Women for America persistently lobbied state congressmen in Iowa to ensure that the Equal Rights Amendment did not pass in that state. We won because of the commitment of Iowa women whose lives would have been directly affected.

Our government was created and intended to provide a foundation of laws and guidelines upon which Americans could freely live as they desired. But our society has become captivated with the idea that men and women and all different cultural groups are alike. Interest groups, such as the American Civil Liberties Union (ACLU), work diligently to ensure that states and communities each live according to the broadest measure of the laws of our nation, in order to ensure that all states and communities live alike.

GOD, KINGS, AND PRESIDENTS

Throughout the 1980s and early 90s, Christians enjoyed the presidencies of two men who were committed to the pro-life movement and pro-family causes. Not everyone agreed with their economic policies, but Christians appreciated the fact that both men stood up for the rights of parents, children, and the unborn. During this period, I think we Christians had a tendency to sit back and relax, feeling comfortable that the president would take care of controversial matters. We were wrong to let down our guard.

We are never to trust a leader in place of trusting God. In 1 Samuel we read the account of Israel, who demanded to have a king like the neighboring pagan nations:

> So all the elders of Israel gathered together and came
> to Samuel at Ramah. They said to him, "You are old,
> and your sons do not walk in your ways; now appoint a
> king to lead us, such as all the other nations have."
>   But when they said, "Give us a king to lead us," this
> displeased Samuel; so he prayed to the LORD. And the
> LORD told him: "Listen to all that the people are say-
> ing to you; it is not you they have rejected, but they
> have rejected me as their king." (1 Samuel 8:4-7)

When Samuel warned the people of their poor choice in
wanting a king in order to "be like the other nations," the
obstinate people refused to listen.

> "When that day comes, you will cry out for relief from
> the king you have chosen, and the LORD will not
> answer you in that day."
>   But the people refused to listen to Samuel. "No!"
> they said. "We want a king over us. Then we will be like
> all the other nations, with a king to lead us and to go
> out before us and fight our battles." (1 Samuel 8:18-20)

The children of Israel were warned, but they chose to forsake the Lord anyway. They wanted a king to fight their
battles for them. Does all this sound familiar? Are we also
seeking a government that can eradicate all of life's struggles—something tangible, something we can behold with
our eyes? We should learn from the Israelites that we
should not expect a president, a king, or a government to
solve our problems.

When a nation is righteous, the citizens of that nation
are blessed. Similarly, when the majority in a democratic
nation chooses evil over good, even the righteous suffer for
the prevailing evil. When our courts will not allow our public schools to have prayer, Bible reading, teaching of cre-

ation, or anything that has any reference to God, our nation will suffer the consequences. "Righteousness exalts a nation," the Bible tells us, "but sin is a disgrace to any people" (Proverbs 14:34).

WOMEN OF ACTION

What characteristics should we look for in those we choose to represent us at different levels of government? This is important for all of us to consider. On the average, barely half of the American electorate vote in a presidential election. We care enough to gripe but not enough to vote for candidates we can trust to lead our country. As Christian women we need to be alert to the political process. We cannot expect to have leaders who are aware of our desires and needs if we do not even vote.

Many Christians have begun to think that they have no place in politics—that God and the state have nothing to do with each other. But we are called to make God's name known in all that we do, and politics affects our lives. We compromise our faith when we fail to fulfill our duties and exercise our rights as citizens in voting, and when we vote solely on the basis of our economic situation rather than on moral issues. The economy is important, but it is certainly a secondary issue when the very fiber of our country is being ripped apart due to the carelessness with which we treat our social problems.

Because government affects all our lives, we need to make our voices heard. In 1977 India Edwards wrote:

> Women have made enormous strides in the last decade, but they still do not seem to understand what a power they could be if they took more interest in government on all levels. If they realized how much government affected their lives and those of their children, they could not resist having a stronger voice in the affairs of

the nation, the states, and their home communities. We are not a minority but we still are treated as though we were one, and a small one at that.[5]

We traditional women are a tremendous power in this country, and if we don't stand up to say who we are and what we want for our families, someone else will speak for us. Chances are, it will be a feminist. The so-called women's movement is well schooled in the ways of government and is a powerful force to which politicians in Washington, D.C., and all over America pay attention, knowing that the alternative is risking feminist protests.

Christian women must be women of action. As author Connie Marshner wrote,

> Christian political energy must focus clearly, consistently, and relentlessly on protecting motherhood. Restoring motherhood to a position of honor and value must be the priority underlying all other political alliances and judgments. Averting the attack on the heart of the family must not be an incidental add-on to a list of political concerns; it must be fundamental to Christian political involvement.[6]

GOVERNMENT AGAINST THE PEOPLE

Government, which is intended to be "by the people" and "for the people," often enforces policies that are *against* the people. Marshner cites the following as evidence of the government's bias against the family:

- the economic attack on the family through the tax code
- the subsidization of the institution of social parenthood
- the destruction of the family as a viable economic unit by the diminution of men's wages

■ the attack on motherhood by no-fault divorce, which
effectively robs motherhood of its last protection,
marriage

With the ever-enlarging role of government in the raising of our children, we must ask ourselves if our children
belong to us or to the government. In this age where to be
"politically correct" often necessitates being morally cor-
rupt, the thought that ultimate authority for raising children might rest in the hands of the government is alarming
to any thoughtful adult.

The rights of God-fearing parents are receding even as
you read this. Yes, our nation was founded upon biblical
truths, and the preservation of our nation is predicated
upon the upholding of these biblical principles, but the religious liberties of Christians are diminishing daily, as are
those of the family at large. We are, I'm afraid, living in a
post-Christian era. We must render to Caesar (the government) the things that are Caesar's (taxes and honor), but
we are also to render to God the things that are God's—our
lives and those of our children (Matthew 22:21).

GRANDDADDY GOVERNMENT

Statistics show that there is a gender gap in politics.
Women and men want different things from government.
Women typically want a bigger government than men
because as women we crave security, stability, and the assurance that someone will provide for and protect us. That
"someone" used to be our fathers and husbands, but as the
American family has eroded, women have transferred their
trust from men to government. All the while our trust
should have been in the Lord.

Government is hardly a cure-all. In an article discussing
the view of government held by the three presidential candi-
dates in the 1992 elections, journalist Bruce Fein wrote:

Responses by the trio uniformly either accept or champion a government obligation to eliminate virtually all of life's misfortunes, discomforts, and unpleasantness. . . . One seemed to suggest that all human defects or evil could be avoided if the government offered a nanny to hug and kiss every child during its initial 18 months of life.[7]

Statistics indicate that women's number one concern is the economy. "How will I survive?" women seem to be asking. In a society that has turned its back on God—transferring its trust from God to man—it seems the next natural transfer is from man to government. Where else would one turn?

Mothers are naturally concerned about the welfare of their children. Thus the issue of child care takes a prominent place in women's thinking. "Who will care for the kids, since I can't?" we seem to be asking. The obvious answer to many is "Granddaddy Government." Subconsciously we fool ourselves into believing that Granddaddy Government owns everything, when in fact, he *owes for everything!* We are burdening Granddaddy Government, who can't even afford to pay rent, with responsibilities that we ourselves ought to be meeting. The saying "You get what you pay for" works both ways—we also "pay for what we get!" We are paying dearly for Granddaddy Government's "help." Our "liberation" from the home has turned around to bite us in the pocketbook and in the heart.

Family leave has become an important women's issue. If mothers were permitted to be at home with their children, who *desperately* need them—not just for a few weeks after childbirth, but all during their growing-up years—we would not need Granddaddy Government to baby-sit for us while we're at work.

But like the proverbial donkey following a carrot, women

keep on the employment track, thinking that just around the corner is a pot of gold. Even if we reach the stated goal of earning equal wages and having equal responsibilities in the workplace as men, I'm afraid we will find we have been pursuing fool's gold all along. Calling on Granddaddy Government to help us every time we think we spy a bully on the employment playground will not solve our problems.

Women, do you see that you and I, as well as the rest of our nation, have turned our back on God, our Provider, Protector, and Judge? "The pious were wrong to think that a kingdom not of this world could be ushered in by a temporal kingdom," wrote Cal Thomas.[8] He was right. We have been looking to the visible, the tangible, the here-and-now government to be our "almighty," when we should have been looking to God alone. Only God can provide the help, protection, and security we need.

"THE YEAR OF THE WOMAN"
Was 1992 really "The Year of the Woman" in politics? It would be more accurate to say that it was the year of the "progressive-Democratic-woman-who-supports-abortion-rights." Groups such as EMILY (Early Money Is Like Yeast) and the National Women's Political Caucus provided significant assistance in elevating many pro-abortion women to positions of power in 1992.

Patricia Ireland, president of the National Organization of Women, noted that the "Year of the Woman" referred only to the most visible results of a winning strategy. Ireland explained that the strategy, begun a decade earlier, was flooding the election with candidates. Anita Hill, "the media's patron saint of sexual harassment,"[9] added fuel to the feminist fire when she testified before the Senate Judiciary Committee to keep Judge Clarence Thomas off the Supreme Court. The result was explosive.

And what do these "victors" have to say about their victories? Jane Danowitz of the pro-abortion Women's Campaign Fund comments: "The Republican party should look back and realize it has wasted its most valuable resource by not putting forward more pro-choice women."[10]

It appears that some do not realize that that which seems politically expedient is not always eternally profitable. As Christians, we live for the final results, not easy victories. We dare not turn our backs on the innocent babies headed for abortion. We know that we will ultimately be victorious, whatever setbacks we may encounter along the way.

The National Organization for Women and other women's organizations can be expected to push for a number of "women's issues," particularly now that their appetite for control and power has been whetted. We can look for them to fight in support of continued abortion on demand, women in combat, and lesbians in the military, as well as numerous other issues that undermine American families. And they will never be content, but will always demand more.

OUR RELIGIOUS ROOTS

It must be remembered that the Constitution was not written in a religious vacuum. Most of the writers of the Constitution were Christians or held to Christian moral principles. James Madison, the chief architect of the Constitution, explained the nature of the American Republic in these words:

> "We have staked the whole of all our political institutions upon the capacity of mankind for self-government, upon the capacity of each and all of us to govern ourselves, to control ourselves, to sustain ourselves according to the Ten Commandments of God."
> It was never the intention of the framers of the Constitution to develop a document that would prohibit

people from governing themselves according to the Law of God. The Constitution's purpose was to protect those Christian rights, not to prohibit citizens from freely exercising their religious beliefs.[11]

Our Constitution begins with these words:

> We the People of the United States, in Order to form a more perfect Union, establish Justice, insure domestic Tranquility, provide for the common defence, promote the general Welfare, and secure the Blessings of Liberty to ourselves and our Posterity, do ordain and establish this Constitution for the United States of America.

Our founding fathers knew that the success of our nation depended greatly upon the moral uprightness of its citizens. Never did the framers of the Constitution envision that the government they were establishing would one day serve as a national benefactor catering to the whims of a morally decrepit citizenry!

HOW LOW CAN WE GO?

It is tragic that our government stoops so low as to allow the destruction of its young potential citizens. Can we expect God's blessing upon a government that sheds innocent blood as part of its policy? Our nation's government was established, not to dictate individual politics, nor to promote special interests, but to liberate its constituents to pursue life, liberty, and happiness. Our government was to free its citizens to live before God in good conscience and to pursue their life objectives with as few strings attached as possible. The citizens, and not the government, would accept responsibility for their actions. If an individual made an investment that succeeded, he would reap the rewards; if it failed, he would suffer loss. Life would be experienced at full impact.

As it is, however, our government artificially shields us from joy and pain. Gary DeMar warns us about the dangers of governmental dependency:

> If citizens do not become aware of the intended bibli-
> cal function of civil government, two things will hap-
> pen. First, individuals, families, churches, and schools
> will lay aside their God-ordained responsibilities. The
> result will be that the civil government with its ever-
> growing bureaucracy will take on the responsibilities
> reserved for the citizens at the expense of the free-
> doms. Second, those who function in the realm of civil
> government will tyrannize and exploit the governed by
> controlling their lives with laws never meant to be
> used by the civil authorities.[12]

Author Charles Sykes, who has recently written *A Nation of Victims: The Decay of the American Character,* makes these observations on the imbalance of our nation:

> It is no accident that voters have consistently elected
> people who promise to cure every ill without ever pre-
> senting them with a tab. Our politics thus merely reflects
> our lives. Americans have come to believe they are enti-
> tled to all sorts of self-realization, gratification and fulfill-
> ment—without strings, pain or responsibility.[13]

Another point of grave concern is our government's ten-
dency to treat criminals like diplomats while enslaving the victims of crime to a life of fear and injustice. Writes the prophet Isaiah:

> Woe to those who call evil good and good evil, . . . who

acquit the guilty for a bribe, but deny justice to the
innocent. Therefore, as tongues of fire lick up straw
and as dry grass sinks down in the flames, so their
roots will decay and their flowers blow away like dust;
for they have rejected the law of the LORD Almighty
and spurned the word of the Holy One of Israel.
(Isaiah 5:20, 23-24)

THE JUDEO-CHRISTIAN TRADITION
On the hot issue of separation of church and state, the
First Amendment to the Constitution, added in 1791, was
intended to protect religion from influence by the state,
not vice versa! Erwin W. Lutzer wrote the following in his
book *Exploding the Myths that Could Destroy America:*

> In our Constitution familiar words appear: "Congress
> shall make no law respecting an establishment of reli-
> gion, or prohibiting the free exercise thereof." Clearly,
> the intention was (1) to limit the power of federal gov-
> ernment by ensuring that it would not establish a state
> church, then (2) it was not to prohibit the free exer-
> cise of religion. . . .
>
> The fathers of this nation never dreamed that
> separation of church and state meant that God should
> be separated from government. The government build-
> ings in Washington bear ample testimony to the belief
> that faith in God is the basis for establishing laws and
> running the affairs of a nation.
>
> For example, the Ten Commandments hang over
> the head of the chief justice of the Supreme Court
> (would that they had been read before the infamous
> *Roe v. Wade* decision of 1973). In the rotunda the
> words "In God we trust" are engraved, and on the
> Library of Congress we have "The heavens declare the

glory of God and the firmament showeth His handi-work."[14]

Former U.S. Secretary of Education William J. Bennett gives the following brief historical overview, clearly showing the inextricable relationship between church and state in our developing nation:

> The story of America is the story of the highest aspirations and proudest accomplishments of mankind. To understand those achievements, we must understand the religious roots from which they sprang. We must tell our schoolchildren about the Puritans, who founded a "city upon a hill" with a sacred mission: to be a beacon unto the nations and to lead a community of saints to the New Jerusalem; about Benjamin Franklin, who proposed that the Great Seal of the United States depict Moses leading the chosen people from the wilderness to the Promised Land; about Abraham Lincoln, who saw the Civil War as a divine punishment for the sin of slavery; . . .
>
> Everyone, including agnostics and atheists, must concede that the Judeo-Christian tradition is a major formative influence on American life, ideals and principles.[15]

SALT, LIGHT, AND PRAYER

Christians are called to be the salt of the earth and the light of the world. Our personal standards of obedience to God's commands are to have an effect on our community. Our light is to shine freely and unobstructed.

"You are the salt of the earth," Jesus told his disciples.

> But if the salt loses its saltiness, how can it be made salty again? It is no longer good for anything, except

to be thrown out and trampled by men. You are the
light of the world. A city on a hill cannot be hidden.
Neither do people light a lamp and put it under a
bowl. Instead they put it on its stand, and it gives light
to everyone in the house. In the same way, let your
light shine before men, that they may see your good
deeds and praise your Father in heaven. (Matthew
5:13-16)

Unfortunately, the majority of Christian women have
been "saltless" citizens, having little influence on the righteousness of our nation. We have been quiet and unin-
volved, while the feminists have aggressively promoted
amorality and humanism. It is time for Christian women in
our nation to become aggressively "salty" in prayer and
action as we work to restore moral standards and an acknow-
ledgment of God's Word as truth in America.

The key to moral prosperity in a nation is not found in
politics as usual—"capturing the other side's general,"[16] as
Chuck Colson put it—but in the individual development of
holiness. As you obey God, you affect me, and as I obey
God, I affect others, and inevitably they do the same. There
is no shortcut to moral health. It can only be accomplished
one by one.

One of God's charges to Christians is that they pray for
their authorities. It is not a debatable command:

I urge, then, first of all, that requests, prayers, interces-
sion and thanksgiving be made for everyone—for
kings and all those in authority, that we may live peaceful and quiet lives in all godliness and holiness. This is
good, and pleases God our Savior, who wants all men
to be saved and to come to a knowledge of the truth.
(1 Timothy 2:1-4)

God desires that Christians pray so that the gospel might be freely shared. Ultimately, the eternal state of men and women is the most important thing in life. Are you consistently praying for the leaders in your life? As responsible children of God and as citizens of our nation, it is our duty to intercede for our authorities.

Action follows prayer. As James wrote, faith without works is dead. A natural consequence of faith is action. I would urge you to become active in a local Concerned Women for America prayer and action chapter. You can contact our headquarters for information on how to do so. The encouragement of fellow intercessors cannot be overstated.

We should look to the Lord as we consider our government. God wants his people to look first to him for the provision of our needs. No other person or institution can meet our needs as he can. As the Bible tells us in Psalm 118:8-9:"It is better to take refuge in the LORD than to trust in man. It is better to take refuge in the LORD than to trust in princes."

Good presidents come and go; God alone remains the same. Whoever our elected officials may be, whether we agree with them or not, as Christians we are called to pray for them. We must constantly keep in mind that the one in whom we trust and to whom we will one day give an account is God himself. "For the LORD is our judge, the LORD is our lawgiver, the LORD is our king; it is he who will save us" (Isaiah 33:22).

We are living in dangerous but exciting times. While there is yet liberty, while we still have the freedom to pray and act and vote, let us be wise. Let us make the most of every opportunity. The days are evil, but through the strength of our heavenly Father, you and I can stand against the oncoming darkness.

QUESTIONS
FOR REFLECTION AND DISCUSSION

1. What are some practical ways in which women can exercise godly influence on government policy?
2. What are the intended biblical functions of government?
3. What are different types of government that exist, and what roles are they to play in our lives?
4. Do you agree with the opinion that our country has become "a nation of victims"?
5. What can a woman reasonably expect out of civil government?
6. What can women do to encourage government to be pro-family?
7. Why is it important to pray for our government authorities?
8. Was the First Amendment to the Constitution separating church and state intended to protect the church from the state or the state from the church?

OUR
GREATEST
*D*ESIRE

12

We Want to Be Women of God

Have you ever played the "Who Am I?" guessing game with a child? The child pretends to be a person, and you ask questions: "Are you real or fictional? Living or dead? Human or animal?" Sometimes the game gets quite complicated! If you've ascertained that the *who* is a cartoon animal, you'll be reduced to asking, "Do you like to eat carrots or road runners?"

In real life as in this game, we have to know who we are to know what we really want. And when the world is constantly reevaluating and redefining the role and worth of women, it's sometimes difficult to know who we were meant to be. We need to compare God's teachings to what the world tells us. Whether you are a young mother, an older single career woman, or a retired grandmother, you need to discover *who you are* as a woman and *what God created you to be.*

CREATED WOMAN

We are *women of God.* We were created by him. It is our desire to understand his purposes in creating us and to live in a manner worthy of him. Women who have a personal relationship with Jesus Christ know him in a very real way.

God created all persons—men and women—as unique individuals. He did not intend for us to hate each other or to envy others' unique characteristics, but to learn from and love each other. We are to help one another and value the gifts and talents of others as well as our own. In our differences, we are to form complementary relationships.

Women were created with very different characteristics from those of men. We are known for our nurturing capability and have traditionally filled roles in society that suit our more gentle qualities. Traditionally women have chosen careers in education, nursing, and service, or they have volunteered for charity work. But prevailing opinions espoused by feminists have pushed women into careers ranging from the priesthood to military service. I hope women will rediscover the qualities that make them uniquely different from men, so we can feel good about how God made us.

I like the way Phyllis Schlafly begins her book *The Power of the Positive Woman*. She says a woman's life, faith, behavior, and potential for fulfillment are all determined by her attitudes about who and why she is. The positive woman, says Schlafly,

> understands that men and women are different, and that those very differences provide the key to her success as a person and fulfillment as a woman. The woman's liberationist, on the other hand, is imprisoned by her own negative view of herself and of her place in the world around her. This view of women was most succinctly expressed in an advertisement designed by . . . NOW. . . . The advertisement showed a darling curly-headed girl with the caption: "This healthy, normal baby has a handicap. She was born female." This is the self-articulated dog-in-the-manger, chip-on-the-shoulder, fundamental dogma of the women's libera-

tion movement. Someone—it is not clear who, perhaps God, perhaps the "Establishment," perhaps a conspiracy of male chauvinist pigs—dealt women a foul blow by making them female.[1]

God's Word has much to say about the worth of a woman. Proverbs 31:10-31 tells us that the godly woman doesn't fit the worldly image of the woman who's "come a long way, baby!" and earned the right to hang a cigarette out of her mouth in public or to straddle the bar stool and order a beer. Instead, she is a woman of great worth not only in her home, but in her community. She feeds and clothes her family and helps the poor; she is involved in business and is wise in her teaching. Her husband adores her, her children call her blessed, the community respects her. She's as fulfilled in her role as she can be, and she's proud—not bitter—to be a woman!

THE RESTLESS WOMAN

How different is this woman from the "restless woman" of today! The restless woman listens to the lies of the world and chafes under what she considers limitations. Women of God accept the challenging, unique, and rewarding role God has designed for them.

Restless women don't know what to do with their lives. Women of God know who and what they are.

A restless woman has no idea of what—or *whose*—she is. A restless woman may be married and not want to be a housewife or mother. Often what she sees on television or reads in women's magazines tells her that she's "trapped" or "unproductive" if she stays at home. She justifies choosing work over her children by reasoning that her career boosts the family's economic status—they have a better home, they entertain more, the kids have Nintendo. Surely those things make up for the hours that she's away! After all, many of her friends have "escaped" from home and are working full-time. They wear nice clothes as they go on business trips and carry leather attaché cases. Their lives are so much more rewarding and glamorous than the lives of women who are mere housewives. Career success, status, style—don't these things make a woman happy? According to feminist philosophy, they should.

WHAT DO RESTLESS WOMEN WANT?

Several years ago I read a newspaper article recounting a meeting of the National Council of Jewish Women in Nashville, Tennessee. The keynote speaker, Shirley Leviton, presented a speech titled, "What Does a Woman Want?" In her speech, however, she declared that she had no answers: "Even though I've been researching the feminine soul for the thirty years I've been active in the NCJW," Leviton said, "I've not yet been able to answer the question of what women want."[2]

That's not very encouraging. This *woman* has been studying women for thirty years, yet she's just as befuddled as Freud was. She's not alone in her confusion; other women are saying the same thing. Judith M. Bardwick, a feminist, has written one of the fairest and most honest analyses of the women's problem I've seen. In the first chapter of her book *In Transition,* she candidly admits, "I have no prescriptions for happiness."[3]

While people from opposite ends of the ideological spectrum agree that women are generally unsure of themselves and uncertain of their futures, there is much disagreement on the cause and cure for women's restlessness. In *The Feminine Mystique,* Betty Friedan writes:

> The problem lay buried, unspoken, for many years in the minds of American women. It was a strange stirring, a sense of dissatisfaction, a yearning that women

suffered in the middle of the twentieth century in the
United States. Each suburban wife struggled with it
alone. . . . "Is this all?" . . . I could find no peace, until I
finally faced it and worked out my own answer.[4]

Betty Friedan asked the right questions, but she found
the wrong answers. She implies that the answers to women's
problems are found in self-made solutions. Granted, this
may be the only logical conclusion an atheistic or agnostic
woman may reach. But while Christian women may observe
the same sense of dissatisfaction and questions about worth,
we should find a different answer to our inner struggles. We
will find answers when we look beyond ourselves to our
heavenly Father.

The most persistent problem women face today is simple
spiritual hunger. It is the cause of the gnawing, yearning
unrest in the hearts of today's women. This anxiety has
caused many fine Christian women to compromise their
spiritual convictions because when their hearts were restless
they went to the wrong source for help. Centuries ago,
Saint Augustine gave us the answer to spiritual hunger in
this prayer: "You have made us for yourself, and our heart is
restless until it rests in you."

The feminist looks into a woman's heart for answers; the
humanist looks into human nature; the Christian looks to
Christ. You and I were created with what the philosopher
Pascal referred to as a God-shaped vacuum. This void can
be filled only by a personal, close relationship with Jesus
Christ. The sense of restlessness in our world today is God's
way of drawing women to himself.

TWENTIETH-CENTURY EVE
What if Eve were your next-door neighbor? Eve was
restless in those early days of Creation, and if she lived
today it's likely she'd be caught up in the confusion facing

women today. She might not be among those women who march down Pennsylvania Avenue in front of the White House demanding attention, their "rights," and their choices, but she might be wondering about where she fits into the changing role of women. Would she feel inferior and second-rate for staying home with Cain and Abel?

What if Eve were sitting with her family in your church? Would she listen to the wise and loving instruction from the Lord who created her, even though the pastor's words seemed to conflict with her own human reasoning and the advice she gleaned from the television talk shows? Would she hear God's voice or fall prey to the voices all around her shouting, "Do what seems right in your own eyes!"

In the midst of the beautiful garden God created, Eve made the mistake of listening to the crafty serpent rather than listening to God. Satan convinced her that God would not punish her for disobeying his authority, and after looking at the fruit and deciding it was good, pleasant, and desirable, she acted on Satan's deceitful suggestion. That choice estranged her from the presence of the Lord, and she and her husband hid themselves in the Garden. The Lord pronounced a curse on them as he had warned them, and he drove them from the Garden of Eden. Eve lost her innocence and her joy. She and her family paid a high price for choosing their own way.

GOD'S DESIGN

Why is there so much confusion over what women really want? To put it simply, some women are still listening to the voices of deceit, and as a result, women do not know who they are. The voices of the liberal media continually tell us that women should be treated as if they were the same as men, that pregnant women should have the "right" to reject their unborn babies from their reproductive organs, that men are obstacles to women, and that women must learn to live without men or at least without dependency upon them.

These ideas are at odds with God's original purpose in creating man and woman. In Genesis we read that after God created Adam in his own image and placed him in the Garden of Eden, he saw it was not good for man to be alone and decided to make a helper fit for him. God then created woman. He brought the woman to Adam that they might be joined as husband and wife and become one flesh. That was the beginning of God's plan for the family.

Eve was designed to help Adam in the same way that God has helped men and women throughout human history. In her book *Woman Liberated,* Lois Gunden Clemens explains:

> Woman brings to man a human relationship through which he becomes a more complete person. No other living creature could provide such companionship for him; there had to be one who was like himself and yet distinct from him. This implies that man and woman were not meant to be two independent, self-subsistent individuals having no need of each other. Rather, they are made to be one dual being in a totality consisting of two distinct persons. . . . Each one is a correlated component naturally oriented toward the other.[5]

Belief in creation does not undermine our position as women. It empowers us, for we are unique and have special qualities that complement the distinctive qualities of men. Women and men were made to complete each other mentally, spiritually, emotionally, and physically.

We stand beside men as unique creations, and we stand before God as individuals, not as men or women. Jesus spoke equally to men and women, giving the same commands, warnings, and promises to each. "Does this not mean that Christ was placing woman's human personality on the very same level as that of man?" Lois Clemens asks. "As moral beings responsible to God, man and woman are not subordinated in any manner. Jesus saw woman's worth as residing in her own person, rather than in her relation to man."[6]

The Bible tells us "there is neither Jew nor Greek, slave nor free, male nor female, for you are all one in Christ Jesus" (Galatians 3:28). God's redeeming relationship with humankind extends equally to men and women. In him, we are all the same. But in our human relationships, we can rejoice in our differences. We can find fulfillment in our roles as women of God.

FEMINISM AS RELIGION

Ultimately, dedicated feminists reject belief in one God and substitute a belief in many gods. "In moments of sorrow or joy," writes Gloria Steinem,

> too many of us are forced to turn to ceremonies that falsely elevate some and demean others, that separate us from nature, that make us feel ashamed of sacred parts of ourselves. It will take courage, creativity, and community to replace them with inclusive ceremonies that mark life passages; rituals that externalize universal myths and nature's symbols of old and continuing mysteries—and exclude no one. But . . . all religions still have within them some tradition of listening to an inner voice and therefore acknowledging the sacred worth of each individual and of nature. As new archaeological discoveries and ways of carbon dating them show, the last 5,000 to 7,000 years of patriarchy, monotheism, and racism are a brief moment in the vast progression of human history.[7]

Desperately seeking affirmation, restless women pattern themselves after the "prophets" of their movement. Feminist role models such as Simone de Beauvoir, Betty Friedan, Gloria Steinem, Germaine Greer, and Susan Faludi provide poor models of happiness and fulfillment, and yet somehow they are placed upon intellectual pedestals as though all women should emulate them.

We don't need more confused, haranguing feminists. Our nation needs women of God with the courage to stand up for what is right. Being a woman of God does not mean being a "church mouse"—squeaky and always underfoot. Being women of God means that we derive our strength and energy from God and act as the loving managers of our families. Being women of God means that we know how and why we were created. Being women of God means that we have personal, deep relationships with Jesus Christ and serve him in our God-designed roles.

NEW AGE GODS

"Just as women achieve new heights in business and politics, modern women are fascinated with the mythology of the 'Goddess Reawakening,'" write Patricia Aburdene and John Naisbitt in *Megatrends for Women.* "Meanwhile feminist theologians reject the notion that divinity is somehow male and are reinterpreting Scripture to reclaim women's spiritual heritage."[8]

Patricia Aburdene and John Naisbitt define the goddess movement as "a mixture of Wicca, the New Age, feminism and mythology."[9]

We shouldn't be surprised to see the connection of Wicca (witchcraft), the New Age, feminism, and mythology. They all have one thing in common: Self. They are all dedicated to empowering Self, avenging Self, and promoting Self. The more we learn of each of these destructive practices, the more clearly we see their source is not wisdom but unfettered folly.

Paul warns us:

> Mark this: There will be terrible times in the last days.
> People will be lovers of themselves, lovers of money,
> boastful, proud, abusive, disobedient to their parents,
> ungrateful, unholy, without love, unforgiving, slander-
> ous, without self-control, brutal, not lovers of the
> good, treacherous, rash, conceited, lovers of pleasure
> rather than lovers of God—having a form of godliness
> but denying its power. Have nothing to do with them.
> (2 Timothy 3:1-5)

I can almost hear you saying, "Come on now, Beverly,
really. *Goddess worship?* Today?" To see where authors
Aburdene and Naisbitt are coming from, we must understand the basic nature of the New Age movement. First, the
term *New Age* is a misnomer. It is anything but new. Its doctrines have afflicted mankind since the beginning of time.
The basic New Age doctrine is the same line the old serpent
fed Eve back in the Garden—"You can be like God!" Make
no mistake, the New Age movement is nothing short of
ancient paganism in splashy celebrity packaging.

Like you, I find it perplexing that modern, "enlightened"
women are turning to such an irrational faith. Even
Aburdene and Naisbitt acknowledge that this trend in
women to revalue the "nonrational," as they put it, is one of
the main reasons "the Goddess commands recognition
today"![10] In their book we learn that a goddess course
called "Cakes for the Queen of Heaven" has been adopted
by some Methodist, Congregational, and Episcopal groups,
as well as by an order of nuns!

Satan just doesn't quit, does he? The New Age movement
is dangerous and is spreading rapidly in many insidious
forms. Though it may not always be labeled "New Age," you
can spot the foundation of New Age religion in feminist

doctrine that rejects men and denounces the male-dominated institutions of our society, especially in religion.

> Women of the late 20th century are revolutionizing
> the most sexist institution in history—organized reli-
> gion. Overturning millennia of tradition, they are chal-
> lenging authorities, reinterpreting the Bible, creating
> their own services, crowding into seminaries, winning
> the right to ordination, purging sexist language in lit-
> urgy, reintegrating female values, and assuming posi-
> tions of leadership.[11]

"Male-dominated institutions from the U.S. Senate to the hierarchy of the Roman Catholic Church will be dragged kicking and screaming into the 20th century," write Aburdene and Naisbitt.[12] Still need convincing that goddess worship is a serious religion? Listen to another quote from *Megatrends for Women:*

> The collective memory of the Goddess is reawakening
> as millions of women acknowledge their power, experi-
> ence freedom from male domination, and channel
> sweat and creativity into transforming the world.
> Whether a woman espouses traditional religion, New
> Age spirituality or atheism, her sense of personal
> power is enhanced by the mythology of the Goddess,
> which awakens confidence, belonging and self-
> esteem.[13]

We can observe several things from the above passage: First, goddess worship is clearly linked to feminism; goddess worship is not merely a personal belief system but has its eye on world transformation; goddess worship is infecting "traditional religion" (certain Christian denominations); and finally, goddess worship lures unsuspecting followers with promises of boosted confidence, belonging, and self-esteem.

As if hypnotized by the prospect of global worship of a female deity, the authors write: "The Goddess is associated with reverence of the earth and its environment. Her image is reemerging. . . . The Goddess influences all humanity."[14]

Paul warned Timothy of the emergence of just such a deadly doctrine at the end of the age: "The Spirit clearly says that in later times some will abandon the faith and follow deceiving spirits and things taught by demons" (1 Timothy 4:1).

The growing obsession with environmentalism stems from the worship of Mother Earth, and we have all been affected by this influence. At this point in our country, reverence for the earth and animals is greater than reverence for men and women. As I write this, it is illegal to disturb the nests of bald eagles and endangered turtles but perfectly legal to rip unborn babies from their God-designed "nests."

A female-based religion awaits the world, say Aburdene and Naisbitt. In New-Age-style goddess worship, not only has the deity exchanged genders, but so have the spiritual leaders.

THE POWERLESS GODDESS

As women seek the desires of their hearts, will they find their answers in a religion designed and led by females? How does "goddess worship" fulfill a woman's needs and build lasting self-esteem on a practical, day-to-day basis? Women are looking for a spiritual guide to help them when they cannot help themselves. A religion that is built around Self, such as New Age religions, can never completely fill that God-shaped vacuum inside every man and woman. Our inner emptiness can be filled only by the Lord Jesus Christ.

False gods may offer a temporary experience that satisfies Self for a short time, but they cannot sustain women through life's traumas. When a woman stands at the graveside of a loved one, how can a pagan goddess comfort her? When a husband turns his back on his wife of thirty years for a younger woman, can a Self-based religion heal her broken heart without poisoning her with anger toward all men? If a teenager commits suicide, what can the New Age gods offer his heartbroken mother during the long nights ahead?

When a woman experiences comfort, love, and security from the God who created her and gave his one and only Son to be her Savior, she has found the only lasting relationship that gives her the confidence to know who she is and to whom she belongs.

KNOWING GOD

Women want to know God, and the way we come to know him is through his Son, Jesus Christ. "Jesus answered, 'I am the way and the truth and the life. No one comes to the Father except through me'" (John 14:6). Through Christ, we can learn about the nature of God and get to know him as any close friend, but this happens only when God reveals himself to us. Jesus said, "Whoever has my commands and obeys them, he is the one who loves me. He who loves me will be loved by my Father, and I too will love him and show myself to him" (John 14:21). In other words, if we are sincere in our pursuit of God, he will reveal more and more of himself to us.

God delights in our desire to know him. We see this beautifully portrayed in the story of Esther in the Old Testament. She is an example of a woman who grew in her knowledge of God as the circumstances of life—specifically the likely annihilation of the Jews in Persia—demanded faith and courage. After fasting and seeking God's face, she was given the wisdom, favor, and power to turn the fate of her people from imminent death to life and exaltation. This young woman's growing knowledge of God manifested itself in humble confidence and quiet strength.

Knowing God is the greatest experience you or I could ever hope to achieve. These timeless words of Jeremiah speak to us clearly today:

> This is what the LORD says: "Let not the wise man boast of his wisdom or the strong man boast of his strength or the rich man boast of his riches, but let him who boasts boast about this: that he understands and knows me, that I am the LORD, who exercises kindness, justice and righteousness on earth, for in these I delight," declares the Lord. (Jeremiah 9:23-24)

As we begin to know God and understand his ways, we will also see and experience his loving-kindness and his fair and judicious hand. As women, we can cherish and appreciate these attributes of God that give us strength and confidence. So we see that what women really need is simply to know God. God has our best interests at heart in all he does.

GOD'S GREAT MERCY

God is not only loving, just, and righteous, but he is also gracious and merciful. It is these attributes that make it possible for him to love us and care for us. How blessed we are that he is this way! Without his mercy and grace he would be justly inclined to avoid our company and ignore us altogether. As it is, however, we enjoy the delightful role of being God's "objects of mercy" (Romans 9:23)—evidence of God's goodness and compassion toward those deserving his wrath.

God is also a forgiving God. Regardless of the deeds we may have done in the past, his mercy is everlasting, and his love is beyond measure. "The Lord is not slow in keeping his promise, as some understand slowness. He is patient with you, not wanting anyone to perish, but everyone to come to repentance" (2 Peter 3:9). Because God wants us all to repent and come to him, he has promised that "if we confess our sins, he is faithful and just and will forgive us our sins and purify us from all unrighteousness" (1 John 1:9).

Regardless of what we may have done—aborted a baby, committed adultery, entertained selfish ambitions, exploded in anger, or whatever—God is willing to forgive if we call upon him. When we receive his forgiveness and salvation, we become part of God's family. "Yet to all who received him, to those who believed in his name, he gave the right to become children of God" (John 1:12).

THE FATHER'S LOVING DISCIPLINE

As our loving Father, God is constantly overseeing and leading us. We often require his correction in our lives. But knowing we might resent his discipline and fail to recognize his kind intentions, God has told us in his Word that we need and will receive his correction if we are his children. God disciplines us to change us.

When we first yield our lives to God, we give him our base and unattractive human natures, but as we learn to know him, we begin to take on some of his characteristics. We will be filled with the fruit of the Holy Spirit. His concerns and desires will become ours. As God cares for the helpless, we will do the same. We will love others as God has loved us. We will more clearly discern right from wrong.

Galatians 5:16-23 tells us that if we walk in the Spirit, we will experience love, joy, peace, long-suffering, kindness, goodness, faithfulness, gentleness, and self-control. What woman would not desire these attributes? This is what fulfills a woman and builds her strength and quiet confidence through Christ.

When we enter into a relationship with God through Jesus Christ, we come to know God's love. In a world filled with self and hatred, we can demonstrate God's love because we know him and have received him. As some secular women continue to build a wall of hatred against men, we can learn to love and respect men because of God's love through us. The Scriptures tell us: "If anyone acknowledges that Jesus is the Son of God, God lives in him and he in God. And so we know and rely on the love God has for us. God is love. Whoever lives in love lives in God, and God in him" (1 John 4:15-16).

WE WANT TO KNOW MORE ABOUT GOD

The Old Testament tells us that "the name of the LORD is a strong tower; the righteous run to it and are safe" (Proverbs 18:10). It also gives us the example of trusting God rather than our own devices. "Some trust in chariots and some in horses, but we trust in the name of the LORD our God" (Psalm 20:7).

As Kay Arthur points out in her excellent book *Lord, I Want to Know You,* in biblical times a person's name often represented his character, attributes, and nature. With that understanding, we can see how the names of God prove his character to us. Studying the names of God is not a mere academic exercise useful only to theologians. Far from it; it is very practical and deeply encouraging to contemplate the names by which God has chosen to call himself in his Word. We know God is a provider and a guide, but as we study his names, these characteristics come alive.

Yahweh-rapha: The Hebrew word *rapha* means to mend, cure, heal, repair, and make whole. God does that according to his will for us. It is Yahweh-rapha who mends our heartaches, restores our broken lives, and heals our diseases. God, our healer, sustains our lives and makes us whole in every way—physically, spiritually, mentally, and emotionally. Speaking to his people after their departure from Egypt, God said: *I am the LORD who heals you* (Exodus 15:26). Just as God created our lives, skillfully forming us in the womb (Psalm 139:13-17), so he sustains and maintains our lives. The Great Physician is a faithful and powerful friend.

El Elyon: God is the sovereign ruler of all the universe. Do you really believe that? Would you believe it if you had been rejected by your husband and your child had turned in rebellion against you? In those times it is particularly important to realize that God has not forgotten you and that he is still powerfully involved in your life! "Who among you fears the LORD and obeys the word of his servant? Let him who walks in the dark, who has no light, trust in the name of the LORD and rely on his God" (Isaiah 50:10).

In trying times it can be extremely difficult to understand and believe that God is working all things out for our good. When life seems to be falling apart and there is no light at the end of the tunnel, it is important that you and I fix our eyes upon Jesus and remember his promise to always be at work in our lives. Think of Joseph, who consoled his brothers when they feared that he would execute them for their treachery toward him years earlier. Joseph assured them that he understood that what they meant for evil, God meant for good (Genesis 50:20).

When others disappoint us, fail us, betray us, and work out evil schemes against us, do we trust in the name of the Lord, the sovereign ruler of the universe who is actively working all things together for our good? If we do, we will be strong. "You will keep in perfect peace him whose mind is steadfast, because he trusts in you" (Isaiah 26:3).

El Shaddai: Our all-sufficient one pours out his blessings upon our lives. He longs to meet our every need. Paul knew this well: "And my God will meet all your needs according to his glorious riches in Christ Jesus" (Philippians 4:19).

When money and friends are scarce, it's comforting to know that God's eye is on the sparrow and on us as well. The single mother can know that God will supply her needs. God knows what you need, and he is a generous provider.

Adonai: The Lord and Master of the universe requires full allegiance to his will. "Jesus is Lord" is not just good bumper sticker material—it must be a reality in our lives. Jesus asked, "Why do you call me, 'Lord, Lord,' and do not do what I say?" (Luke 6:46).

In another passage of Scripture, God says: "'A son honors his father, and a servant his master. If I am a father, where is the honor due me? If I am a master, where is the respect due me?' says the LORD Almighty. 'It is you, O priests, who show contempt for my name'" (Malachi 1:6). If Jesus is not the master of your life, he is not your Lord.

Yahweh-jireh: The LORD will provide. *Jireh* means "to see." The meaning implied in the name Yahweh-jireh is that God foresees—he knows in advance what we need and makes provision for us. He knows when a child will be born with Down's syndrome, and he will provide for the parents and the child. What a comfort it is to know that nothing—absolutely nothing—catches God off guard. He knows and he will provide for our every need no matter how small!

Yahweh-shalom: The LORD is peace. In this age of widespread confusion and heartache, it is wonderful to have an unchanging, immutable source of peace. "Great peace have they who love your law, and nothing can make them stumble" (Psalm 119:165). One of the many names that describe our Lord Jesus in Isaiah 9:6 is "Prince of Peace." He reigns over all with peace. He has told us: "Peace I leave with you; my peace I give you. I do not give to you as the world gives. Do not let your hearts be troubled and do not be afraid" (John 14:27). Even when there is conflict in the family, the Lord has promised to provide peace. The world's peace is based on circumstances that change as quickly as the weather. God's peace is based on his steadfast commitment to us and our good.

Yahweh-raah: the LORD, my Shepherd. Sheep are not the most brilliant of animals. They have been known to calmly walk off a cliff. Sheep have virtually no skills for self-defense, and they blindly follow the crowd. They need a shepherd. And so do you and I! As David sang in Psalm 23, "The LORD is my shepherd, I shall not be in want." Our heavenly Shepherd leads us, restores us, accompanies us, corrects us, feeds us, and blesses us with joy. With God as our Shepherd, we truly shall not want.

You and I instinctively look to the here and now. But if we want to be women of God, we would do well to consider the end of our lives. Before we know what has happened, we will reach the conclusion of our allotted time on earth.

Do you know with great confidence that you will be well received when you stand face to face with God, the final judge of all mankind? Is your eternal destiny secure? Of all the blessings God has given us, eternal life is by far the greatest. In Psalm 23, David wrote, "Surely goodness and love will follow me all the days of my life, and I will dwell in the house of the LORD forever" (Psalm 23:6). Are you able to say that?

ASSURANCE OF SALVATION

God's Word tells us that we can be certain that we can be forgiven for all our sins. We can know that when we die we will be with the Lord. "I write these things to you who believe in the name of the Son of God so that you may know that you have eternal life" (1 John 5:13). What a comfort and assurance it is to know that we can be entirely forgiven for all of our moral failures, given a clean slate, and welcomed into heaven.

It is by the grace of God, through faith in Christ, that all people—regardless of their past sins—can be saved. Salvation is the gift of God, not the result of our efforts, so that none of us could ever boast (Ephesians 2:8-9). In heaven we will never hear any boasting about our good deeds; instead, we will boast in the name of the Lord our God!

> If you confess with your mouth, "Jesus is Lord," and believe in your heart that God raised him from the dead, you will be saved. For it is with your heart that you believe and are justified, and it is with your mouth that you confess and are saved. As the Scripture says, "Anyone who trusts in him will never be put to shame." For there is no difference between Jew and Gentile—the same Lord is Lord of all and richly blesses all who call on him, for, "Everyone who calls on the name of the Lord will be saved." (Romans 10:9-13)

Finally, Jesus says, "Here I am! I stand at the door and knock. If anyone hears my voice and opens the door, I will come in and eat with him, and he with me" (Revelation 3:20). Women of God rejoice because Christ has brought us eternal salvation and the comfort of his presence now and in time to come.

Phillip Keller writes beautifully of the joy of companionship with God in his book *God Is My Delight:*

> Coming to him boldly but reverently, we know we will not be spurned or turned away. If in utter integrity, without pretense, we place ourselves in his care, he in turn imparts himself to us. This is true and valid communion with our Father which brings both him and us enormous delight.
>
> As I move softly now, down the twilight path of my earthly pilgrimage, these joyous and gentle encounters with my Heavenly Father are the most precious inter-

ludes. These are times to be savored with intense satisfaction. For as I entrust myself and all that pertains to my little life to His care, his assurance comes to me, "Yes, my child, all is well. I am here with you. Be of great courage. Be of good cheer!"[15]

That is what being a woman of God is all about—entrusting ourselves into God's care, regardless of what happens to us in life, and knowing that he cares for us and will provide for us. Being a woman of God provides the greatest satisfaction and fulfillment a woman could ever desire.

It *is* possible for an American woman in the last years of the twentieth century to find the desires of her heart, even when traditional values are under attack and God's truth is challenged on all sides. David lived in a time like ours, and this is what he wrote:

> Do not fret because of evil men
> or be envious of those who do wrong;
> for like the grass they will soon wither,
> like green plants they will soon die away.
>
> Trust in the LORD and do good;
> dwell in the land and enjoy safe pasture.
> *Delight yourself in the LORD*
> and he will give you the desires of your heart.
> (Psalm 37:1-4, italics mine)

QUESTIONS
FOR REFLECTION AND DISCUSSION

1. What is the root cause of restlessness in women?

2. What does it mean to be a woman of God?

3. Why have some in our society turned away from God to "goddess" worship?

4. How does having a vibrant relationship with God sustain women in difficulties?

5. In addition to salvation, what does a relationship with God offer women?

6. Which of God's attributes do you cherish the most?

7. How essential is it for a woman to cultivate a growing relationship with God?

8. What are some ways in which a woman is called to honor God in her life?

Notes

Come Walk with Me . . .

1. Quoted by Dee Jepsen, *Women: Beyond Equal Rights* (Waco, Tex.: Word Books, 1984), 15.
2. Phyllis Schlafly, *The Power of the Positive Woman* (New Rochelle, N.Y.: Arlington House Publishers, 1977), 73.
3. Jepsen, *Beyond Equal Rights*, 51.

Chapter 1: We Want Happiness and Significance

1. David G. Myers, *The Pursuit of Happiness: Who Is Happy—and Why?* (New York: William Morrow and Company, 1992), 19.
2. Quoted by John Piper, *Desiring God: Meditations of a Christian Hedonist* (Portland, Oreg.: Multnomah Press, 1986), 173.
3. *The Quotable Woman*, ed. Running Press staff (Philadelphia: Running Press), 394.
4. Quoted by Sheldon Vanauken, *A Severe Mercy* (New York: Harper & Row Publishers, 1977), 208.
5. Susan Faludi, *Backlash: The Undeclared War against American Women* (New York: Crown Publishers, Inc., 1991), xvi.
6. Faludi, *Backlash*, xvii.
7. Myers, *The Pursuit of Happiness*, 41.
8. Myers, 148.
9. Myers, 21.
10. Myers, 21.
11. Barbara Tuchman, "Mankind's Better Moments," Jefferson Lecture, Washington, D.C., April 1980, quoted in *The New York Public Library Book of 20th Century American Quotations* (New York: Warner Books, 1992), 19.
12. William Raspberry, "The Power of Spirituality," *The Washington Post*, 7 December 1992, 2.
13. Thomas Szasz, *The Second Sin*, 1973, quoted in *20th Century American Quotations*, 341.
14. Vivian Gornick, University of Illinois *Daily Illini*, 25 April 1981.

15. Robert S. McGee, *The Search for Significance* (Houston, Tex.: Rapha Publishing, 1990), 11.

16. Jepsen, *Beyond Equal Rights,* 79.

17. Anne Ortlund, *Disciplines of the Heart: Tuning Your Inner Life to God* (Waco, Tex.: Word Books, 1987), 65.

18. Jepsen, *Beyond Equal Rights,* 179.

19. Pearl S. Buck, speech to the U.S. House of Representatives, 16 January 1941, quoted in *20th Century American Quotations,* 497.

20. Elisabeth Elliott, "Whose Am I?" *Moody Monthly,* May 1980, 40.

Chapter 2: We Want Meaningful Friendships with Women

1. Myers, *The Pursuit of Happiness,* 147–148.

2. Myers, 143.

3. Myers, 144.

4. Margery D. Rosen, "All Alone: The New Loneliness of American Women," *Ladies Home Journal,* April 1991, 216.

5. Deborah Tannen, *You Just Don't Understand: Women and Men in Conversation* (New York: William Morrow and Company, 1990), 17.

6. Tannen, *You Just Don't Understand,* 24.

7. Naomi Rhode, *More Beautiful than Diamonds: The Gift of Friendship* (Nashville: Thomas Nelson Publishers, 1991), 63.

8. Quoted by Rhode, *More Beautiful than Diamonds,* 62.

9. Quoted by Rhode, 57.

10. Stevenson, Burton, ed. (taken from *Essays, First Series: Friendship*) *The Home Book of Quotations* (New York: Dodd, Mead & Company, 1967), 727.

11. Quoted by Rhode, 60

12. Rhode, 55.

Chapter 3: We Want Respect and Honor from Men

1. Faludi, *Backlash,* xvi.

2. Myron Magnet, "The American Family, 1992," *Fortune,* 10 August 1992, 43.

3. Elisabeth Elliot, *The Shaping of a Christian Family* (Nashville, Tenn.: Thomas Nelson Publisher, 1992), 171.

4. Elliot, *The Shaping of a Christian Family,* 171.

5. John Piper and Wayne Grudem, *Recovering Biblical Manhood &*

Womanhood: A Response to Evangelical Feminism (Wheaton, Ill.: Crossway Books, 1991), 35.

6. Anne Moir quoted by Karen S. Peterson, "Debate: Does 'Wiring' Rule Emotion, Skill?" *USA Today,* 8 July 1991, 1A.

7. Associated Press, "Landmark Result: Women and Men Do It Differently," *The Washington Times,* 4 June 1992.

8. Moir quoted by Peterson, "Debate," 1A.

9. Karen S. Peterson, "New Rules Make Men Underdogs in Game of Love," *USA Today,* 31 July 1992.

10. Tannen, *You Just Don't Understand,* 24.

11. Tannen, 17.

12. Tannen, 16.

13. Piper and Grudem, *Recovering Biblical Manhood,* 36.

14. Piper and Grudem, 36.

15. Piper and Grudem, 39.

16. Piper and Grudem, 39.

17. Piper and Grudem, 36.

Chapter 4: We Want Purpose and Examples

1. Ellen Goodman, "Reunion of the Ungeneration," *Washington Post,* June 1988, quoted in *20th Century American Quotations,* 297.

2. Judith Bardwick, *In Transition* (New York: Holt, Rinehart & Winston, 1979), 2–3.

3. Bardwick, *In Transition,* 21.

4. Letha Scanzoni and Nancy Hardesty, *All We're Meant to Be* (Waco, Tex.: Word Books, 1975), 207.

5. Bardwick, *In Transition,* 17.

6. Tim LaHaye, *The Battle for the Family* (Old Tappan, N.J.: Fleming H. Revell, 1982), 143.

7. Betty Friedan, *The Feminine Mystique,* quoted in *20th Century American Quotations,* 297.

8. Albert Einstein, *New York Times,* 20 June 1932.

9. Burton Yale Pines, *Back to Basics* (New York: William Morrow, 1982), 157.

10. Connaught C. Marshner, *The New Traditional Woman* (Washington, D.C.: Free Congress Research & Education Foundation, 1982), 3.

11. George H. Gallup, Jr., and Timothy Jones, *The Saints among Us: How the Spiritually Committed Are Changing Our World* (Harrisburg, Pa.: Morehouse Publishing, 1992), 19.

12. *The Nineteenth Century, A Documentary History* (San Francisco: Harper & Row, 1981) vol. 1, *Women and Religion in America*, 2.

13. *The Nineteenth Century,* 242.

14. *The Nineteenth Century,* 322.

15. Frances Willard, *Glimpses of Fifty Years: The Autobiography of an American Woman* (Chicago: H. J. Smith & Company, 1889), 611.

16. Edward E. Bok, ed., *Success and How to Win It* (New York: The University Society, 1902), 318.

Chapter 5: We Want to Be Fulfilled Single Women

1. Jane Gross, "Divorced, Middle-Aged and Happy: Women, Especially, Adjust to the 90s," *New York Times,* 7 December 1992, A14.

2. "Singles: Dealing with Sexuality," Focus on the Family radio broadcast, 1992.

3. Audrey Lee Sanders, *Single and Satisfied* (Wheaton, Ill.: Tyndale House Publishers, 1971), 25.

4. Eugenia Price, *God Speaks to Women Today* (Grand Rapids: Zondervan Publishing House, 1969), 77.

5. Gien Karssen, *Getting the Most Out of Being Single: The Gift of Single Womanhood* (Colorado Springs, Colo.: Navpress, 1983), 136–137.

Chapter 6: We Want to Love and Respect Our Husbands

1. Piper, *Desiring God,* 172.

2. Piper, *Desiring God,* 192.

3. Lawrence J. Crabb, Jr., *The Marriage Builder* (Grand Rapids: Zondervan Publishing House, 1982), 21.

4. Barbara Vobejda, "Baby Boom Women Setting Divorce Record," *The Washington Post,* 9 December 1992, A1–A8.

5. Vobejda, "Baby Boom Women" A1–A8.

6. James C. Dobson, *Straight Talk to Men and Their Wives* (Waco, Tex.: Word, 1980), 21.

7. Virginia Fugate, *On the Other Side of the Garden: Biblical Woman-*

hood for Today's World, (Tempe, Ariz.: Alpha Omega Publications, 1992), 93.

8. Tim and Beverly LaHaye, *Spirit-Controlled Family Living* (Old Tappan, N.J.: Fleming H. Revell Company, 1978), 174.

9. Crabb, *The Marriage Builder,* 34.

10. Tim and Beverly LaHaye, *The Act of Marriage: The Beauty of Sexual Love* (Grand Rapids: Zondervan Publishing House, 1976), 11.

11. Richard and Mary Strauss, *When Two Walk Together: Learning to Communicate Love and Acceptance in Your Marriage* (San Bernardino, Calif.: Here's Life Publishers, 1988), 100.

12. Steve Farrar, *Point Man: How a Man Can Lead a Family* (Portland, Oreg.: Multnomah Press, 1990), 167.

13. Elliott, "Whose Am I?" 41.

14. F. LaGard Smith, *What Most Women Want: What Few Women Find* (Eugene, Oreg.: Harvest House Publishers, 1992), 33–34.

15. Farrar, *Point Man,* 78.

16. Fugate, *On the Other Side of the Garden,* 87.

17. Fugate, 87–88.

18. Fugate, 89.

19. Fugate, 95.

20. Fugate, 97.

21. Elliott, "Whose Am I?" 41.

Chapter 7: We Want to Experience the Beauty of Motherhood

1. Randy Alcorn, *Pro Life Answers to Pro Choice Arguments* (Portland, Oreg.: Multnomah Press, 1992), 39.

2. Quoted by R. C. Sproul, *Abortion: A Rational Look at an Emotional Issue* (Colorado Springs, Colo.: Navpress, 1990), 115.

3. Quoted by Angela Bonavoglia, *The Choices We Made* (New York: Random House, 1991), 99–100.

4. Sproul, *Abortion,* 39.

5. Sproul, 97.

6. Mona Charen, "Putting Children at Risk at the Family Frontier," *The Washington Times,* 25 June 1992.

7. As quoted by Christina Hoff Sommers, "Feminism and the College Curriculum," *Imprimis* 19, no. 9, (1990):3.

8. Brenda Hunter, *Home by Choice: Facing the Effects of Mother's Absence* (Portland, Oreg.: Multnomah Press, 1991), 16.

9. Hunter, *Home by Choice*, 26.

10. Hunter, 28.

11. Elizabeth Snead, "Fonda Basks in Luxury of Staying Home," *USA Today*, 3 September 1992.

12. Hunter, 100.

13. Magnet, "The American Family," 46.

14. Louis S. Richman, "Struggling to Save Our Kids," *Fortune*, 10 August 1992, 34.

15. Quoted by Magnet, 46.

16. Connaught Marshner, *Can Motherhood Survive: A Christian Looks at Social Parenting* (Brentwood, Tenn.: Wolgemuth & Hyatt Publishers, Inc., 1990), 66.

17. Marshner, *Can Motherhood Survive*, 65.

18. Thomas Sowell, "Working Overtime to Hide a War," *The Washington Times*, 12 October 1992.

19. R. C. Sproul, *Lifeviews: Understanding the Ideas that Shape Society Today* (Old Tappan, N.J.: Fleming H. Revell Company, 1986), 23.

20. John Leo, "A Shove Beyond Tolerance," *The Washington Times*, 12 August 1992.

21. Leo, "A Shove Beyond Tolerance."

22. Leo, "A Shove Beyond Tolerance."

23. Leo, "A Shove Beyond Tolerance."

24. Judy Mann, "What's So Bad about Abstinence?" *The Washington Post*, 24 April 1992.

25. Magnet, "The American Family," 47.

Chapter 8: We Want Joy and Satisfaction in Our Work

1. Booker T. Washington, *Up from Slavery*, 1901, quoted in *20th Century American Quotations*, 506.

2. Judith Martin, *Common Courtesy*, 1985, quoted in *20th Century American Quotations*, 519.

3. Susan Caminiti, "Who's Minding America's Kids," *Fortune*, 10 August 1992, 53.

4. Caminiti, "Who's Minding America's Kids," 53.

5. Hunter, *Home by Choice*, 62.

6. Edith Mendel Stern, "Women Are Household Slaves," *Ameri-*

can Mercury, January 1949, quoted in *20th Century American Quotations,* 579.

7. Hunter, *Home by Choice,* 78.
8. Phyllis McGinley, *Sixpence in Her Shoe,* 1964, quoted in *20th Century American Quotations,* 519.
9. Barbara Bush, address to 1990 Graduating Class, Wellesley College, Wellesley, Massachusetts, 1 June 1990.
10. Nancy J. Perry, "If You Can't Join 'Em, Beat 'Em," *Fortune,* 21 September 1992, 59.
11. Kathleen Cooper, quoted by Perry, "If You Can't Join 'Em," 59
12. "Work and Family: Exploring New Options," *The Family in America,* September 1992, 1.
13. Carolyn Lochhead, "The Yoke of Preferential Policies," *Insight,* 25 June 1990, 22–24
14. Perry, "If You Can't Join 'Em," 59.
15. Perry, 58.
16. Perry, 58–59.
17. Teresa Godwin Phelps, "Pollyanna, Alice, and Other Women in the Law," *Notre Dame Journal of Law, Ethics & Public Policy* 6, no. 2 (1992):289.
18. Jepsen, *Beyond Equal Rights,* 50.

Chapter 9: We Want Truth from the Women's Movement

1. *20th Century American Quotations,* 502.
2. Christine Hoff Sommers, "Feminism and the College Curriculum," *Imprimis* 19, no. 9 (1990):2.
3. *20th Century American Quotations,* 504.
4. Faludi, *Backlash,* xvi.
5. Repplier, Agnes, *Points of Friction,* quoted in *20th Century American Quotations,* 503.
6. *20th Century American Quotations,* 503.
7. Faludi, *Backlash,* 401.
8. Quoted by Sommers, "Feminism," 3.
9. Quoted by Mary A. Kassian, *The Feminist Gospel: The Movement to Unite Feminism with the Church* (Wheaton, Ill.: Crossway Books, 1992), 43.
10. *20th Century American Quotations,* 504.
11. Quoted by Sommers, "Feminism," 2.

12. Gloria Steinem, *Revolution from Within: A Book of Self-Esteem* (Boston: Little, Brown, and Company, 1992), 294.

13. Quoted by Jane Gross, "Does She Speak for Today's Women?" *New York Times Magazine,* 1 March 1992, 38.

14. Kassian, *The Feminist Gospel,* 225.

15. Quoted by Piper and Grudem, *Recovering Biblical Manhood,* 395.

16. Quoted by Kassian, *The Feminist Gospel,* 225.

17. *20th Century American Quotations,* 139.

18. Frank Norris, *The Responsibilities of the Novelist & Other Literary Essays,* 1969, quoted in *20th Century American Quotations,* 140.

19. *20th Century American Quotations,* 140.

Chapter 10: We Want to Find Our Rightful Place in the Church

1. Quoted in *The Encyclopedia of Religious Quotations,* ed. Frank S. Mead (Old Tappan, N.J.: Fleming H. Revell, 1965), 79.

2. Charles Colson, *The God of Stones & Spiders: Letters to a Church in Exile* (Wheaton, Ill.: Crossway Books, 1990), 92.

3. Kassian, *The Feminist Gospel,* 217.

4. Carleton R. Bryant, "Ordain Women and Gays, Says Episcopal Bishop," *The Washington Times,* 30 July 1992.

5. Steinem, *Revolution from Within,* 313.

6. Scanzoni and Hardesty, *All We're Meant to Be,* 171.

7. Dr. Ray Pritchard, "Men and Women in Biblical Perspective" (Calvary Memorial Church, Oak Park, Illinois), October 18, 1992.

8. John MacArthur, *God's High Calling for Women* (Chicago: Moody Press, 1987), 29.

9. Pritchard, "Men and Women in Biblical Perspective," 18 October 1992.

Chapter 11: We Want Our Desires Respected by Government

1. Gary DeMar, *God and Government: A Biblical and Historical Study,* vol. 1 (Atlanta: American Vision Press, 1982), 29.

2. Montesquieu, *De l'Esprit des Lois,* bk. viii, ch. 1.

3. Woodrow Wilson, speech, New York Press Club, 9 September 1912.

4. "What America Believes: The Rest of the Story," Select Com-

mittee on Children, Youth, and Families, U.S. House of Representatives, October 1990, 3.

5. India Edwards, *Pulling No Punches,* 1977, quoted in *20th Century American Quotations,* 394.

6. Marshner, *Can Motherhood Survive?* 229.

7. Bruce Fein, "Sign of U.S. Spiritual Decay," *The Washington Times,* 21 October 1992.

8. Cal Thomas, "The Torch and the Flame," *The Washington Times,* 20 October 1992.

9. Brent Bozell, "Prepping Anita for Sainthood," *The Washington Times,* 20 October 1992.

10. "Female Ranks in Elected Jobs Get a Big Boost: Numbers Grow in Both State and U.S. Offices," *The New York Times,* 8 November 1992.

11. Quoted by DeMar, *God and Government,* 137–138.

12. DeMar, *God and Government,* 59.

13. Charles J. Sykes, "I Hear America Whining," *The New York Times,* 2 November 1992.

14. Erwin W. Lutzer, *Exploding the Myths that Could Destroy America* (Chicago: Moody Press, 1986), 160–62.

15. William J. Bennett, "Divine Guidance for Young Scholars," *The Washington Post,* 27 October 1992.

16. Quoted by Gustav Niebuhr, "Religious Right Hopes Clinton Swells Ranks: Democrat in White House May Fire Up Conservatives," *The Washington Post,* 8 November 1992.

Chapter 12: We Want to Be Women of God

1. Schlafly, *The Power of the Positive Woman,* 11.

2. Quoted by Virginia Keathley, "She's Still Searching for Women's Soul," *The Tennessean,* 13 April 1980, 4E.

3. Bardwick, *In Transition,* 8.

4. Friedan, *The Feminine Mystique,* 15, 70.

5. Lois Gunden Clemens, *Woman Liberated* (New Canaan, Conn.: Keats Publishing, 1975), 12.

6. Clemens, *Woman Liberated,* 22.

7. Steinem, *Revolution from Within,* 309.

8. Patricia Aburdene and John Naisbitt, *Megatrends for Women* (New York: Villard Books, 1992), xx.

9. Aburdene and Naisbitt, *Megatrends,* 245.
10. Aburdene and Naisbitt, *Megatrends,* 247.
11. Aburdene and Naisbitt, *Megatrends,* 108.
12. Aburdene and Naisbitt, *Megatrends,* xv.
13. Aburdene and Naisbitt, *Megatrends,* 244.
14. Aburdene and Naisbitt, *Megatrends,* 244.
15. W. Phillip Keller, *God Is My Delight* (Grand Rapids: Kregel Publications, 1991), 71–72.

Find Encouragement and Challenge for a Woman's World in These Tyndale Releases

CAUGHT IN THE MIDDLE
Beverly Bush Smith and Patricia DeVorss   0-8423-0355-3

THE CHRISTIAN WORKING MOTHER'S HANDBOOK
Jayne Garrison   0-8423-0258-1

FRAN & JESUS ON THE JOB *(New! Fall 1993)*
Mary S. Whelchel   0-8423-1226-9

HIGH CALL, HIGH PRIVILEGE
Gail MacDonald   0-8423-1349-4

LET ME BE A WOMAN
Elisabeth Elliot   0-8423-2161-6

WANTING TO FOLLOW, FORCED TO LEAD
Elizabeth Baker   0-8423-8279-8

WINDOW TO MY HEART
Joy Hawkins   0-8423-7977-0